BECAUSE JESUS TAUGHT IT

CHRISTIANITY THROUGH THE EYES OF THE CHURCH FATHERS

FLAME

CONCORDIA PUBLISHING HOUSE · SAINT LOUIS

I dedicate this book to my most precious aunts, Sharon Marie Moore and Jane Ellen Pryor. You two have always functioned as angels for me—God's helpers to carry me along the way. I love you both endlessly.

Published by Concordia Publishing House
3558 S. Jefferson Ave., St. Louis, MO 63118-3968
1-800-325-3040 • cph.org

Manufactured in the United States of America

1 2 3 4 5 6 7 8 9 10 34 33 32 31 30 29 28 27 26 25

PRAISE FOR *BECAUSE JESUS TAUGHT IT*

This sounds like a book about ancient Christianity, but even more than that, it is about *contemporary* Christianity—with its perfectionism and endless self-scrutiny—and our desperate need for the Sacraments. FLAME's joy in discovering the efficacy of Baptism and the real presence of Christ in the Lord's Supper, as found in the church father's works and carried over into Lutheranism, is exhilarating and contagious. This seminary-trained rap star makes an engaging case for a faith that is both evangelical and sacramental. Or, as he calls it, "ancient Christianity as preserved through confessional Lutheran thought."

—**Dr. Gene Edward Veith Jr.,** PhD; author of *Spirituality of the Cross* and *Embracing Your Lutheran Identity*

In his most recent book, *Because Jesus Taught It*, FLAME tells inspiring stories of faith and faithfulness through the ages in ways that speak to our contemporary times. With insights from the earliest Christians as well as his own walk of faith, FLAME challenges readers to explore a deeper understanding of the teachings of Jesus that make a difference in our lives today.

—**Rev. Dr. Gerhard Bode,** chairman of the department of historical theology and director of the Center for Reformation Research, Concordia Seminary, St. Louis, Missouri

Church history, contrary to popular opinion, is far from a mere theoretical academic pursuit. Studying the contexts, writings, and lives of faithful men and women who have gone before us in Christ's church should be a deeply practical and faith-building journey that helps us make sense of our own life experiences and Christian walk. *Because Jesus Taught It* is an illustration of this truth. In a seamless melding of memoir and theology, FLAME brings the reader along on his personal journey of patristic discovery. This study highlights the strengths of the

PRAISE FOR *BECAUSE JESUS TAUGHT IT*

Lutheran theological tradition, equipping those new to Lutheranism and lifelong Lutherans alike to identify the comfort, assurance, and beauty of our confession of faith when contrasted with errors common in American evangelicalism. Deeply relatable and moving, yet informative and researched, FLAME's book on the early church fathers and the historic Christian view of the Sacraments is fresh, well-written, and difficult to put down.

—**Christa Petzold,** author of *Journey Through Church History* and *Gathered by Christ: The Overlooked Gift of Church*

FLAME gets the church fathers—and they got him too. Despite what you may have been taught growing up, Christianity did not go off the rails after the New Testament, only to be rediscovered by Martin Luther. The Holy Spirit has a history, and this book rejoices in that history. The Word of God and the sacramental life have always gone hand in glove. Like Plato's analogy of the cave, Marcus "FLAME" Gray shares his own discovery of this life, bringing his readers along with him to reacquaint them with the great tradition. I highly recommend this book.

—**Rev. Dr. Joel C. Elowsky,** professor of historical theology, Concordia Seminary, St. Louis, Missouri

Because Jesus Taught It by FLAME is an essential guide for anyone seeking to understand and teach the true nature of Jesus Christ. It emphasizes the importance of clear, Christ-centered instruction, ensuring that even the youngest believers can grasp the core tenets of the faith. This book delves into several key themes:

1. **A History Behind the Teachings**: Exploring the origins and development of Christian doctrines.
2. **Church According to the Early Church**: Understanding how the early Christians practiced and organized their communities.

3. **Baptism According to the Early Church**: Examining the significance and practice of Baptism in early Christianity.
4. **The Eucharist According to the Early Church**: Investigating the early church's understanding and celebration of the Eucharist.

By delving into God's Word and the teachings of the early church, this book will help preserve and pass down the Gospel message for generations to come.

—**Rev. Dr. B. Keith Haney,** assistant to the president for Mission, Human Care, and Stewardship, LCMS Iowa District West

As a lifelong Lutheran, I've learned much from FLAME's journey and gained an even deeper understanding of what we believe about Baptism and the Lord's Supper. FLAME gives us a front-row seat to his tussle with Scripture and the early church fathers as he discovers that Lutheran teaching on Baptism and the Lord's Supper isn't European innovation but a preservation of what the earliest Christians taught. This book will foster understanding and dialogue among readers with different views on the Sacraments and is a fantastic resource for lifelong Lutherans, pastors, church workers, and those wrestling with questions about the Sacraments.

—**Michelle Diercks,** author of *Promised Hope: Finding Peace in God's Faithfulness*

CONTENTS

CHAPTER 1

KEEPING IT SIMPLE?

The concept below sounds spiritually mature, but it is not. It is misguided piety that is meant to show off one's singular focus on Jesus, but it falls short. The statement typically goes something like this:

"I don't get caught up in denominations, tradition, or theological debates. I simply follow Jesus and the Bible."

On the surface, this person comes across as spiritually mature, devout, and free of all baggage because they are solely focused on Jesus and the Bible. However, this is not entirely true.

1. You may not think you follow a denomination, but you do. Even if you claim nondenominationalism. If I asked you what you believe about Baptism, for example, your answer would expose what theological tradition you follow. No way around that.

2. You say you only follow Jesus, but you undergo a healthy intake of preaching from your favorite Christian preachers, podcasters, rap artists, authors, and influencers. You trust them to help interpret Jesus' Word for you and to help you process your faith walk. So in fact, you follow others too, as they are following Jesus. Hopefully, they are following Jesus and His Word, rightly understood.

3. Since the Bible was written in three ancient languages and you read yours in your language, you are already subject to translation, transliteration, and

> interpretation, especially if you have a study Bible with notes and commentary for each verse. So it's not simply you and your Bible. It's your Bible as it's been collected and codified, handled and filtered through a strenuous process, packaged for your consumption.
>
> All this to say, you should relax your confidence in your individualism. This notion that it's just you, Jesus, and your Bible is misinformed and unhealthy.
>
> Paul said that the Holy Spirit gave us teachers to build up and unify the Body (Ephesians 4:11–13).
>
> This sets the context for why we must consider the history of the Holy Spirit's teaching of His church. Why we must consider the origins of the Reformation and Dr. Martin Luther's contribution, the apostolic and church fathers, taking us back to the plain meaning of Scripture as best we can.
>
> To dismiss this joyous task and replace it with your private interpretations, your personal relationship with Jesus, and your Bible revelations is a deviation from God's communal and corporate goal for His Body. Which is dangerous.
>
> Let us consider together the historicity and definition of the church and the Word of God and Sacraments. Even if it challenges our contemporary expression.
>
> Amen?[1]

This is one of my classic social media posts. It is a response to a real comment born out of common criticism. On several occasions, commenters have expressed utter disappointment with my shift in focus as a Christian public figure. That small collection of people laments my attention toward the centralizing of the sacramental life

1 Adapted from a Facebook post by the author on February 10, 2024.

that has always defined Christianity, and they long for the FLAME who overtly championed the five-point TULIP (a way of summarizing key teachings of Reformed theology).

They miss the "old FLAME" who limited his verbiage to the cross of Christ, the crucifixion, and the resurrection. They miss when I did not "harp on" Baptism and the Lord's Supper alongside the cross of Christ. For them, the Sacraments—or the sacramental life—are totally foreign language, completely irrelevant and greatly unnecessary, and thoroughly remove the focus from Jesus' finished work on the cross. When talk of the Sacraments leaves my mouth or parts from my pen, they ache over the seemingly insignificant and inconsequential mentioning of the rites.

If you don't know me, allow me to introduce myself. My name is FLAME, also known as Marcus Gray. I am a Christian rap artist who has been on a lifelong journey for biblical truth, and I've found my home in confessional Lutheranism. Critics who once supported me view me as having fallen from great heights. Some even think I've fallen from grace and have embraced false teaching, that I've been drawn away from truth and am now obsessed with propping up Dr. Luther above Jesus. Or worse, in their minds, that I've become Roman Catholic! "Lord, have mercy," they cry. The distance in their minds between Jesus' earthly ministry, culminating in His finished work on the cross, and the ongoing dwelling of God's presence in our lives as expressed in the sacramental life of the church is as vast as the earth is from the sun.

That long sentence you just read is desperately trying to express how shunned and ignored the Sacraments have become in generic expressions of Christianity. All across the world, brothers and sisters have bitten into the rotten fruit of expressions of the Christian faith focused on morality and personal experience. Sacraments have truly become an afterthought or been forgotten altogether. Where the Sacraments do show up in many church denominations that occupy contemporary airspace, they have been so redefined and altered that they are nearly dead.

I get it, though. I by no means am pretending that I've understood the Sacraments rightly for the majority of my time as a believer. Lamentably, I've gone most of my years as a Christian malnourished and underfed of the bread of heaven, at least in the sacramental way God designed. I remember the utter disgust I would experience upon hearing of baptismal regeneration. As I type this right now, I can recall having a physical reaction on my face and in my stomach. I felt something akin to fright and solemn sadness at the mere thought of the ancient truth of baptismal regeneration.

So why did I change my thinking? After visiting the campus of Concordia Seminary, St. Louis, and deciding to move forward with my training there, I ordered the appropriate books to study for my pending test to gain acceptance into the master's program.[2] I got those books in the mail, cracked them open, and began to dive in. Many things rang true and were familiar. Yet the sections on the Sacraments were particularly vexing. While reading, I thought to myself a myriad of times that I could not possibly study at this school. *They may not even be Christians*, I said to myself. I feared. I prayed. I asked God to open my eyes, to give me discernment and a sensitive conscience to recognize if there were harmful falsities being espoused there. Scary.

It's funny. I just went to grab off my bookshelf one of the books that I had to read to test into the program. You should see the highlights, underlines, and snarky comments written on the page.

2 For details of the whole origin story, read my first book, *Extra Nos*.

"Weird." "Huh, that make no sense." "Okay, good point."

All of this is to say that I understand where my critics are and the mindset they have, the mode of defense they reside in. I am not too far removed from the lived experience of the countless good and pious brothers and sisters in the faith out there in the world. They are dear believers who are used mightily by God to love neighbors and contribute much good to their circles of influence. Yet they deny and have denounced ancient Christian teachings on the grounds of conscience.

One important reason for this is because many of them have not even once been presented the opportunity to consider the historic understanding of the Sacraments. They have never, at all, heard talk of it anywhere. Some tremble at even discussing such Sacraments because they get chills to their bones that they are entertaining Roman Catholicism and so avoid any sacramental small talk.

This reflex to avoid talking about the Sacraments comes, in my opinion, from two main desires. One desire is to guard with dear life the teaching of justification by faith alone (rightfully so!), and the other desire is a longing for unity. I was initially confused by the thought that the Christian life is a baptismal reality, a daily dying and being raised to newness of life. Immediately, the way that concept hit my eardrums was that humans contribute to their own salvation. I thought I was hearing that God uses our first act of obedience (Baptism) to save us.

Quite naturally, I bumped up against that notion in defense of the clear biblical proclamation that we are justified, or made right with God, by faith only. After all, Paul was explicit about this in Romans 5:1–2:

> **Therefore, since we have been justified by faith, we have peace with God through our Lord Jesus Christ. Through Him we have also obtained access by faith into this grace in which we stand, and we rejoice in hope of the glory of God.**

Case closed! Therefore, I felt that there was no way Baptism could fit into this picture. In my mind, like many others who are trained in a similar manner, this necessitated a rejection of baptismal regeneration, in the name of defending justification by faith alone. This is one primary reason a person turns a deaf ear to ancient Christian teaching. They believe they are doing God a solid, honoring Him and His Word by resisting Baptism's role in delivering forgiveness.

The second desire, I believe, is a felt one. This desire goes unspoken but is at the core of the initial argument given at the beginning of this chapter. It leads to the belief that debating Sacraments or even discussing them is senseless, secondary to the Gospel, and distracting from the main thing—Jesus Himself.

This, to me, shows that Christians long for unity. For simplicity. We ache for a day when there is no more disagreement among the saints, when we are all finally on the same page and in complete concord with one another. Isn't this what Jesus prayed for? It's recorded in John 17:21:

> **That they may all be one, just as You, Father, are in Me, and I in You, that they also may be in Us, so that the world may believe that You have sent Me.**

By God's Spirit, we all desire this oneness. It is a beautiful desire, one that will be realized on that Great Day! Hallelujah! Meanwhile, we wait with patience for the return of our dear Lord. It appears, however, that some creative minds have found a back entrance into that Great Day already. They found the rear door propped open while an angelic being went to take out the trash, and they snuck in, grabbed a spare key, and now offer entrance into that tranquil place here on earth. That place is known as nondenominationalism.

Nondenominationalism sells itself as a kind of heaven, a place where they have carved away all the fat and have the leanest expression of Christianity. No more theological debates. No more bickering over doctrine and fine points of theology. Just pure bliss. Ease. Harmony. Unity. It brings together Christians who disagree on the Trinity, on the nature of Christ, on the Sacraments, and on church structure. But they all love Jesus, want to live "holy," and desire to do big things for the Lord! "Let's reach the culture," they say. "Let's make Jesus famous!" they shout. "Let's fulfill the Great Commission and take Jesus all over the globe."

Who can argue against that? To do so sounds like you are casting shade over the bright light of the Gospel. Like you are narrow-minded and have lost touch with the main thing. For sure, that can certainly be true if one swings to the other extreme and is only interested in deep theological talk without teaching simply and clearly in a way that impacts the average person dealing with the common trials and difficulties of life. That extreme should be guarded against, no question. Nevertheless, if a community of believers aims to reach the world for the sake of Christ with words and good deeds, shouldn't we know what we believe and why we believe it? Shouldn't we understand what those good deeds do and do not do for our standing before God?

Shouldn't we know who God is? The nature of God's existence? The true nature of Jesus, the Messiah? The difference between God's Law and His Gospel? The nature of these rites He established that have been called the Sacraments? How those Sacraments ought to be enjoyed and applied? If the Sacraments are important enough for Jesus to implement, then we would do right to wrestle with how they have been historically understood and practiced to see where they fit into the Christian life.

Shouldn't we consider what the earliest of saints thought about these matters? We can learn from those who were taught by the apostle John, the longest-standing apostle. We can know what the students of the earliest church fathers taught, those who then conveyed those biblical teachings to another generation. How they understood the Godhead. The nature of Jesus. Justification. Baptism. The Eucharist. Yes, even church structure and the gathering of the saints as they met.

I agree, it is much easier to avoid these topics. It is way more convenient to keep it simple and to simply do good in the world, to hear motivational messages that lift your mood and empower you to work hard, to fulfill your aspirations, and to help the community as much as you possibly can, all with the help of God. It is more comfortable to gather on Sundays and enjoy superb music with a full-out dynamic and enthusiastic worship experience, leaving you full in heart, happy in mood, and hungry to do it all over again next weekend.

However, if all those permissible things are happening on Sunday morning and as a part of church life and culture but pastors and parishioners alike have no understanding of the Trinity, the nature of Jesus, or the Sacraments, then that leaves an emptiness that proves to be more harmful to souls than helpful.

I recall a time I spoke with a youth leader about Jesus. Initially, the conversation was about how good Jesus is, how patient He is, and how He unites His church. Even though we may not all see things the exact same way, Jesus binds us together as a family.

The conversation was rich. It was encouraging. Then, things shifted. The youth leader began to tell a story. While telling the story, he corrected himself about something he thought he had gotten wrong. He said, "Well, I'm not saying Jesus is actually God." To which I replied, "Say that again." I thought maybe I had heard him wrong. He restated it: "I'm not saying Jesus is actually God."

I tried to politely correct him. I said, "You mean you're saying He is actually God, right?" By this point, he paused and appeared a bit confused, asking what I meant. I said, "Jesus is actually wholly God and wholly man, in one person. He is the God-man." From there, he began to hear me out and showed strong interest in further conversation. I was genuinely moved with compassion by how open he was to embracing orthodox Christian teaching. He was not resistant at all. He humbly took in the information and agreed with me that Jesus is God from that point on. It was great brotherly fellowship. We both left encouraged.

I thought about it later that day. I became curious about the criteria for being a youth leader in his circle of Christian influence. I did not fault him but thought more deeply about the leaders in place at his local assembly and even his denomination. Did they know he didn't know Jesus was fully man and fully God? Did they ask? Do they teach that anywhere in the course of their church culture? Do they even affirm Jesus' divinity? Or do they not think it relevant to check when hiring a youth leader, as long as the person is good with teens, still looks youthful and relevant, and can help students live morally upright lives while having fun with them?

And, yes, if you're curious, this was a nondenominational church. A perfect example of what happens when the focus of the church is placed mostly on morality and cultural relevance and not on creeds and confessions. Yes, teach the youth how to live as the baptized, trusting in the finished work of Jesus on the cross and delivered in Baptism. Also teach them the historic creeds of the church so they can rightly orient their morality around the triune God of Scripture and their service toward others as an expression of being a forgiven person freely loved by Jesus, thus able to freely love and serve others.

I submit that it is dangerous to produce morally responsible teens who live piously but don't confess the divinity of Jesus. Their youth leader, and perhaps even the entire church at large, didn't teach them who Jesus actually is. This roots them in self-righteousness and confidence in themselves to gain access to God's heaven. Those people are not in better shape in the end. They might be more moral, but they have not gained any righteousness before Jesus, the God-man, because of it. If any church is not teaching who Jesus is, then it is not doing a good job with its vocation to its community, to the world, or to the universal church. It has become simply a community center contributing needed and praiseworthy good in this broken world that we inhabit. It is not teaching Christian doctrine and therefore not functioning as the Christian Church.

Hear how the church is defined in the simplest of terms by the early reformer Philip Melanchthon in the Augsburg Confession:

> **Our churches teach that one holy Church is to remain forever. The Church is the congregation of saints [Psalm 149:1] in which the Gospel is purely taught and the Sacraments are correctly administered. For the true unity of the Church it is enough to agree about the doctrine of the Gospel and the administration of the Sacraments. It is not necessary**

> **that human traditions, that is, rites or ceremonies instituted by men, should be the same everywhere. As Paul says: "One Lord, one faith, one baptism, one God and Father of all" (Ephesians 4:5–6).**[3]

This is a clear statement on what the church is at its core: "the congregation of saints, in which the Gospel is purely taught and the Sacraments are correctly administered." Jesus is the one who brought the Good News of the forgiveness of sins to the world. Therefore, we ought to be clear on which Jesus we confess, clear on who He is and who He is not. We should teach it so that it can be understood in the simplest way so that even a child can understand what we mean. Jesus is both God and man in one person. The earliest saints were Christ-centered and defended the nature of Jesus against all types of false claims.

So to recap: It isn't realistic to say that you can just focus on Jesus without actually learning or teaching who Jesus is. The church needs to teach the Gospel rightly and administer the Sacraments well. We can make sure we do that by digging into God's Word and by learning what the early church taught, in hopes that those teachings would be passed down from generation to generation. Obviously, one of those most important teachings is knowing who Jesus is (both God and man) and that He died to pay for our sins and make us right with God (justification). This enables us to know exactly why we live differently and love others: not to become holy, but because we already are. We'll dig deeper into this later. While the desire to keep things focused on Jesus and as unifying as possible sounds good, the reflex to avoid talking about certain subjects results in rejecting what Christians have taught from the very beginning.

3 Augsburg Confession, Article 7, paragraphs 1–4. Brackets in original.

By studying the teachings of the church fathers, I also learned that they kept Baptism tied to Jesus' work of regeneration and the remission of sins. Baptismal regeneration is hard for many people to embrace, because they do not think of the Sacraments as the Gospel but as a work, or at least an act of obedience flowing out of faith. These types of people also place more emphasis on a personal conversion experience. I wrote the following post on social media and got a great deal of healthy dialogue going:

> **Don't make your conversion experience your savior. Otherwise, you make yourself the savior.**
>
> **Jesus saves. He delivers the salvation He won for us all by His Word and Sacraments. By the power of the Holy Spirit. Trust, believe, and receive the forgiveness your Savior earned for you on the cross.**
>
> **Even when good Christians are struggling along the way with sin and temptation, they ought to look to Jesus and His finished work for them on a tree.**
>
> **Let us strive; taking one day at a time. Let us live a life of repentance (contrition and faith), by God's might. Not our own might, fueled by the old Adam's energy to save ourselves. Yes, we are constantly dying to sin and rising again to new life, which is our Baptism. A drowning and raising Jesus does to us (Romans 6:1–4). It is the work of God. We are indeed the baptized. This is our identity in Christ.**
>
> **Amen, let us bear fruit in keeping with repentance (Luke 3:8), but ultimately, always looking to Christ's absolution on the cross. "It is finished."[4]**

Because some Christians in the contemporary context have

4 Adapted from the author's Facebook post on January 2, 2024.

turned the Sacraments into outward signs or metaphors pointing to what Jesus did long ago, we are positioned to look to ourselves in a way that is unnatural to Christian history. We now feed our God-given appetite, one that He placed in us, with a meal God has not prepared for us: our own fruit. Rather than feeding on and finding satisfaction in Christ's body and blood given for the forgiveness of sins, in the bread and the wine, we feed on our personal improvement. Rather than finding relief for our souls in the waters of Baptism, we soak in our spiritual growth and ability to climb up the moral ladder toward heaven to find assurance.

Yes, many Christians will affirm justification by faith alone, but we may not be as discerning in tracking down common types of teachings or emphases that attack it and contradict it. These emphases hide out among pop-Christian culture, in podcasts, preaching, and conversation. One example of one of those sneaky teachings that functionally renders the Sacraments meaningless is the emphasis on a "personal relationship with Jesus." For many, personal-relationship language and emphasis is the answer and response to religion being abused. But talk of the Sacraments then gets easily dismissed and swept away in the name of denominational bickering. In the following social media post, I addressed a common theme I hear:

> **"Flame, who cares about denominations? It's all about Jesus and going to heaven. Religion is bad. Stop chasing religion."**
>
> **Thx for posting and for your interest!**
>
> **Your statement appears to be spiritually mature but is not. Respectfully. You're simply parroting back popular churchy sayings.**
>
> **1. We only discuss denominations to the extent that**

> denominations make claims about Jesus, the church, and the Bible. Therefore, we must and it is right to think through what claims are being made by each group. The goal is unity among the saints (John 17:21). We can do this in love and in a kind manner.
>
> 2. Religion is not bad. The Holy Spirit wrote to His church and told us to specifically be religious. In the best way (James 1:26–27). . . .
>
> 3. Amen to a relationship with Jesus, but our faith is *not* a mussy personal thing, but a communal one. . . . The "personal" concept is overused and can be harmful in many ways. . . .
>
> 4. Is Christianity only about heaven? That's an incomplete conclusion that Christianity is only about heaven. God gave us an entire Bible, human existence, a large universe to live in, gifts and talents to enjoy and serve others with, and suffering to grow in our dependence on Him and others.
>
> Seems like God is concerned with loads more for His sons and daughters than only getting into heaven.
>
> Slow down, my friend. Ask more questions.
>
> Thx for posting, though.
>
> God's peace.[5]

There is a major danger in turning Christianity into only a personal relationship with Jesus. Using a personal relationship as the primary metaphor can place the focus more on us and our performance and response. We may attempt to determine our standing with God in any given moment, assessing the health of our relationship with God based on how well we are loving Him back, how busy

5 Adapted from the author's Facebook post on June 20, 2024.

we get doing things for Him to demonstrate our deep and heartfelt love with Him. We might also give God the silent treatment when we feel wronged by Him, displaying the cold shoulder when we don't get our way. These are the games people play in human relationships that we transfer over to our personal relationship with God. Overusing the relationship motif to depict the dynamic of what God is doing in His church can be harmful. It leaves little room to consider what God is doing outside of us, *extra nos*, to His church and reduces the communal focus of our faith, hyperindividualizing it instead.

That unhealthy concentration has a particularly negative impact on the historic usage of the Sacraments. In actuality, the sacramental life is the perpetual state we exist in as the church; it is the way God constantly unites us with Himself, with the heavenly host, and with one another—including those who are no longer with us but present with Him. In short, the Sacraments are the Gospel. They are God at work in His church, healing His children from the curse of sin and death and nurturing us with forgiveness and comfort. With that being understood, then yes, the Sacraments are works. Not our works. Not the works of humankind. Not the work of the Christian. Solely, exclusively, entirely God's work alone.

If you are like I was in 2016, when I heard these things for the first time, you're probably thinking something like "Why didn't anyone tell me this? Why have I never heard of the apostolic and church fathers? Why was I never presented with the opportunity to learn about them or their contribution to Christian thought? Why are there few to zero books written about them for the average churchgoer? No children's books with characters from the early church to color in or to memorize? No devotional books for teens to learn about the church fathers and relatable things from their time and ours? No content for college students to gain an understanding on how to defend the faith in a hostile environment like most of the early church fathers? Little to no Bible study material to assist the elderly on aging and leaving a legacy with your life for the sake of the Gospel and the church?" I didn't realize that some of these things existed; I had never heard about them.

It was a major turning point for me to learn that the church has always understood Baptism to be for the remission of sins, that the apostolic fathers perfectly proclaimed the mystical union of Christ's body and blood in the Eucharist. I spent time studying at four undergraduate Bible colleges and was never offered a course on the church fathers. Not once was I given an assignment, a project, or a research topic that included the early church's teachings on the Sacraments. I never heard a lecture during a class or an assembly that made mention of how the apostolic fathers viewed salvation.

Upon being exposed to it for the first time in my master's program at Concordia Seminary, I was a bit upset. I was caught off guard by it. I didn't know how to process it. Why has the church hidden this from me? Why are Christian institutions hiding things from us? Aren't we paying good money to learn about Christianity and its history? Aren't we here to gain a better grasp on how the Holy Spirit has interacted with His church in the world so as to further establish faith in our hearts and minds? It's simple. It should not be a threat to our training to unearth what the early saints believed.

I recall feelings of distrust. Was there an agenda to redefine Christianity to accomplish some ends that I didn't know about? Who are the decision-makers concerning these things? How do they determine what to tell us and what to not tell us? What else are they hiding? As I sat in class, I remember observing as students volleyed back and forth names, dates, controversies, and conclusions the church fathers had come to. They found relevance from the early writings of the church that helped them process current concerns and controversies. I wanted in! But I felt extremely deprived and malnourished on the matter. I didn't even know where to start. Thankfully, I was registered for a class exclusively dedicated to the study of Athanasius. Big shout-out to the brilliant Rev. Dr. Joel C. Elowsky. I had another class that same quarter on Augustine. Another huge hat tip to Dr. Erik Herrmann. I was just beginning to learn the rich history of the Christian Church, and I thoroughly enjoyed it! When people ask me how I've come to understand Christianity the way that I do, a lot of it has to do with what I learned about what Christians have believed since the beginning. In this book, I hope to share some of that knowledge—and the joy that comes with it—with you.

CHAPTER 2

A HISTORY BEHIND THE TEACHINGS

Here is a caption I wrote on my socials on the subject at hand:

> **Bible colleges, seminaries, Bible studies, and all in Christian education, please expose us pupils to the broad scope of church history. Even factions your tradition disagrees with. This way, later on in life, when detractors show up and expose us to "new things" that are actually "old things," it doesn't send us into crisis. Apostasy even. A plight from which many, unfortunately, never recover. Nevertheless, God is faithful and can draw the vulnerable and fractured ones back to Himself. To the institutions that have been doing so, thank you. Carry on, soldiers.**[6]

The reason this was important for me to write was because many are already skeptical of Christianity and scared to trust voices claiming authority. People are "deconstructing" and aiming to strip Christianity down to its rawest form to see what the church truly is at her core. I'm thinking right now of a handful of people who have fallen away from the faith in recent times for these reasons. I came across a video of a guy who had learned that the church fathers believed in baptismal regeneration. He found this to be particularly frightening and concluded it was grounds to distrust and discredit the origins of Christianity because he had not been exposed to the biblical teaching in our contemporary times. Therefore, he questioned the whole of Christianity and threw it out. Others have

6 Adapted from the author's Facebook post on June 2, 2023.

experienced a similar moment of crisis. For instance, they learn that the church has always held to the doctrine of the Trinity, but they were taught a false view of the Godhead. They then feel deceived and as if they've wasted a lot of precious time in false or "off" teaching. This leads to regret, deep discouragement, and, for some, distrust of clergy altogether simply from being underexposed to historic Christianity from the start.

There are plenty of positive stories, however. Countless brothers and sisters discovered the church fathers at one point and dug deeper, finding the sweet proclamation of the mysteries of God, the Sacraments rightly understood. I am one of those positive outcomes. After my brief moment of discouragement about being underexposed to historic Christianity even while being in the academy for years, I eventually found great comfort and encouragement in considering that there was more to the Sacraments, the visible Word, than I knew. I was comforted discovering that Lutherans were not making these things up but that they were aiming to preserve and protect the doctrines that we gather from the apostles. They consider it a major priority to show the succession of doctrine from the apostles to the early church fathers, all the way to the Lutheran Reformation and through to today.

As a new student at the time, steeped in Reformed theology from the Baptist spectrum, I was inundated with conversion experiences and personal testimonies as proof of regeneration. That's all I knew. The entirety of my time as a human being, I'd only heard people talk about how they became Christians by some major catastrophe or personal epiphany. The degrees of the stories varied, some more dramatic than others. But through some life-altering encounter, people came to Jesus. They turned from their old ways and committed themselves to the Lord. One guy in my high school took his braids out, got a low haircut, started wearing suits every day, and carried a Bible throughout the hallways. To him and most people in my world, that's what it looked like when one gets saved.

I was challenged for the first time ever on this matter while sitting in class on campus at Concordia. I asked a fellow student when he had become a Christian and how it happened. I was expecting at least a small war story. Something about how he used to steal from the candy store and got caught one day, which led to tears and grave sorrow, followed by an invite to youth group by his suburban neighbors who love Jesus. He convinced his mom to let him go with his neighbor friend. She gave him permission because she could at least get a break, finally. He probably went and met a cool youth pastor who used current slang in his talk. They gave an altar call, and he confessed his sin of stealing candy and bam! Jesus came into his heart. From that day forward, he had been walking with Jesus and sharing his faith. Bearing fruit and going on mission trips. Now, here he is! At Concordia studying to be pastor to make this world a better place.

Well, that is not at all what he shared. Not even close. He simply said something akin to "Hmmm, I don't remember exactly. My parents have the exact date of my Baptism, though."

I assumed he didn't understand the question. Maybe my St. Louis accent was too thick. I repeated the question: "How did you become a Christian? How did it happen?"

He replied, "I was baptized as an infant. That's all I know."

I was so confused. Why were we talking about Baptism? Worse yet, baptizing babies? I thought I would give it another shot. Maybe I should state my question in a clearer way.

"How did you get saved?" I asked.

"In my Baptism as a baby," he repeated.

I gave up on him. I turned and asked another guy sitting close by. "Hey, bro, how did you become a Christian?" This showed more promise. I just knew he had a crazy story to tell.

"I was baptized as a baby. I have pictures and everything. My parents saved them," he said.

The levels of confusion were rising to the roof now. Finally, I was struck by a breakthrough question.

I asked them both, "So does everyone here have the same experience—being baptized as a baby?"

They said, "Yep, mostly. I mean, there are some guys here who converted later, but most of us were baptized as infants. Even the majority of the professors," they shared.

"But how do you all know that you are saved?"

"Because of our Baptism," one guy remarked. By this point I was starting to pick up on how they viewed Baptism.

One guy said, "Yeah, this is the way the church has always understood Baptism."

"Aw, okay," I said out loud, thinking these guys were crazy and that the entire school was wrong. Nevertheless, I stayed enrolled because I was curious about the claim that this is how the church has always understood Baptism.

As a Reformed Baptist Calvinist, I had been taught to see only conversion experiences when reading Scripture, nothing of Baptism's role in salvation and certainly nothing related to infant Baptism. The emphasis was on having faith in Jesus as a response to hearing the Gospel. They were certain to teach us that God does a work in the heart first before one can believe, but they taught that this work is only for a select few because God did not send His Son, Jesus, to die for all without exception, unfortunately.

There is a better way, the biblical way, of considering how someone comes to faith. If you are repenting (through contrition and faith) and trusting Jesus to forgive your sins, God has already done a work in you. God is *not* responding to your personal realization that you are wicked and need forgiveness for your evil nature and deeds. God's Holy Spirit called you and turned you to repentance. Forgiveness of sin and faith to believe what Jesus accomplished on the cross—for all people (without exception)—is actually for you, and it is "not a result of works, so that no one may boast" (Ephesians 2:9). By God's Word, He now assures you of these realities in your Baptism and at the Lord's Table. You are now free from the penalty of the Law and free to serve all.

Thankfully, I now know how Baptism, regeneration, conversion, salvation, and assurance all work together. I now see that my bros I sat with that first quarter at the outset of my master's training were correct. They were proclaiming ancient Christianity, the articulation of the faith that continued after the apostles. They conveyed the truths to me that have always caused the saints to find comfort and assurance. The early saints drew much comfort and strength from what God was doing in Baptism and the Lord's Supper.

Sitting near the front of my Lutheran Mind class my first year in seminary, I watched three guys ping-pong back and forth on the topic of church councils. One guy said, "Yep, that's what the Council of Chalcedon said." Another spoke, "For sure, similar to the Council of Ephesus." The third guy added, "Don't forget about the Council of Constantinople and the First Council of Nicaea." I wondered, *Are they speaking in code? Plotting a coup d'état or something?* I watched them talk about these things as if they were common knowledge.

I knew the phrase "church history," but I only thought about it in reference to the Reformation (from the Calvinist and Reformed Baptist perspective, that is). I'd heard Augustine's name tossed around a few times, mostly because of his popular writing *The Confessions of Saint Augustine*, which the Calvinistic circle I ran in used to teach us how to watch our motives and our morals and to be transparent about our sin struggles.

I had heard of Arius the heretic, of Sabellius, another heretic, and a little about the Nicene Creed due to my personal interest in the doctrine of the Trinity. Beyond that, there wasn't an emphasis placed on the early church or the development of Christian life throughout the ages in my previous theological studies.

As that first year continued to unfold, I heard name after name from church history, figures that I had never heard of before. I was learning about how the earliest saints lived and what daily life was like back then. I grew more curious about their challenges and strengths. I wanted to know more. I wanted to know if there were things from then that are still relevant to today's times. I even found it curious that Martin Luther and his fellow reformers referred back to the church fathers. Why were they so important to them?

I came to discover that Dr. Luther wanted nothing more than to preserve the unity of the church and her doctrine. He was not at all interested in dividing the church or bickering with the pope. He wanted to maintain apostolic teaching and nothing else. Therefore, when making a case for the Gospel, the Sacraments, or the church, he was always referencing what the church has always taught. He was careful to put forward the truth that he was not trying to create a new sect or schism but simply repeating back healthy teaching from the apostles, the apostolic fathers, and the church fathers.

I started to relax my skepticism as I saw how far back many of the doctrines went that the Lutherans were championing. Learning the number of years the church has held to certain beliefs caused me to pause and consider more seriously if I had missed things along the way. I remember looking around at the students and the professor, thinking, *Man, they all seem to love Jesus and are serious about their faith. Maybe there's something to this stuff that I should consider.*

These men and women seemed just as committed to the spread of the Gospel and sound teaching as the pious people I knew. They appeared to be devoted to good works and the Christian ethic that my camp values. They prayed, read their Bibles, and even talked about the faith in regular conversation like my bros and I did. They used the same Bible I used. They confessed sin and justification by faith alone, like my friends and associates did. Hmmm, it was hard to ignore those observations. *Maybe there was something to these ancient teachings*, I thought to myself.

Ironically, this is one of Luther's arguments for baptismal regeneration from his Large Catechism:

> **The Baptism of infants is pleasing to Christ, as is proved well enough from His own work. For God sanctifies many of those who have been baptized as infants and has given them the Holy Spirit. There are still many people even today in whom we perceive that they have the Holy Spirit both because of their doctrine and life. It is also given to us by God's grace that we can explain the Scriptures and come to**

> **the knowledge of Christ, which is impossible without the Holy Spirit [1 Corinthians 21:3]. But if God did not accept the Baptism of infants, He would not give the Holy Spirit nor any of His gifts to any of them. In short, during the long time up to this day, no person upon earth could have been a Christian.**

Wow! Such a good and practical argument. He goes on to say,

> **Now, God confirms Baptism by the gifts of His Holy Spirit, as is plainly seen in some of the Church Fathers, like St. Bernard, Gerson, John Hus, and others. These people were baptized in infancy, and since the holy Christian Church cannot perish until the end of the world, the sects must acknowledge that such infant Baptism is pleasing to God. For God can never be opposed to Himself or support falsehood and wickedness, or for its promotion impart His grace and Spirit.[7]**

This was exactly my experience and observation. I could not so easily dismiss that the majority of the students and professors that I met had been baptized as infants and bore Christian fruit. They understood Scripture's themes and centered the Bible around Jesus. They called sin evil and promoted the good. They proclaimed the Gospel freely and called people to receive God's forgiveness by faith. They even emphasized doing good in the world.

7 Large Catechism, Part 4, paragraphs 49–50.

All this was a strong argument for the apostolic teachings of the church concerning the Sacraments. I had to humble myself and admit what I was witnessing added to the validity of their claims. Touché.

CHAPTER 3

CHURCH ACCORDING TO THE EARLY CHURCH

Our dear Lord Jesus died in AD 33. John the beloved, the youngest apostle according to tradition, died of old age—maybe around ninety years old—between AD 98 and 100. Have you ever wondered how Christians lived after the last disciple of Jesus died? How did the Christian message spread? How did people hear about Jesus? Did they meet in houses or megachurch buildings? Did they sing songs and go on mission trips? Were there celebrity pastors who won over large crowds for Jesus? What were the threats that surrounded them? How did they engage the culture and witness to others?

These are the questions I started to wonder about. One of my main curiosities was how people became Christians in the early church. If ancient Christian teaching includes baptismal regeneration, then how did that play out? Let's start there. How did the average non-Christian become a Christian in the first generations after the disciples were all finally reunited with their Lord? Let's look a bit at the world of the second-century saints, their pattern of sharing the Gospel, and what it looked like for a person to join the church.

At this time, Christianity was considered mysterious, a mystery religion. There was little known about this small community of people. Their rites and rituals seemed weird and disturbing to those who were privy to any exposure to this group. There were certainly things to observe about Christians publicly, but not much was known about them during the second century. What was known was that these peculiar people worshiped Jesus, who was crucified under Pontius Pilate.

To be a Christian in the second, third, or fourth century meant that you lived under Roman rule. The Roman Empire dominated a large portion of the world back then, making its presence felt through Roman military might, their culture, their art, and their way of living. A large number of differences in religion and philosophy were tolerated unless it appeared that the group was a threat to peace or Roman rule. Christians were sometimes considered atheists because they would not worship the Roman gods and were accused of cannibalism because of the whispers that began to spread that they ate flesh and drank blood, a misunderstanding about the Lord's Supper. Things changed dramatically in the fourth century. Christianity went from an obscure group of people undergoing sporadic rounds of persecution for disloyalty to Rome to a group that was favored. Constantine converted to Christianity, and under Emperor Theodosius I, by the end of the fourth century, Christianity was the official religion of the Roman Empire.

While the Christians of the early church shared our current concern for learning the faith and sharing the Gospel with others, one difference is the seriousness with which the early church took spiritual warfare and demonic engagement. Today, there seems to be two extremes. In today's Charismatic circles, adherents tend to talk about the devil as if he has equal power with the triune God and are gripped by fear of him, expecting him and his demons to be everywhere and in everything. This extreme provides little rest and assurance in Christ Jesus and focuses more on rebuking the devil and "pleading the blood of Jesus." The other extreme in contemporary times is the tendency to ignore Satan and his demons. Thinking of the devil as having occupied the sinner and needing to be exorcised would be the last thing on the minds of most Christians when calling people to Jesus today. It's as if there is no devil or enemy of the church waging war against God's Word and God's people.

During the first few centuries after Jesus' ascension, the church would have assumed the need to rid a person of demons, partially due to the common practice of idol worship. It would have been commonplace to speak of Baptism as not only ridding the person of sin but also freeing the person's body from the devil. Believers taught that Baptism was protection from the devil's influence.

Once a person showed interest in becoming a Christian, they were in need of instruction, in keeping with Jesus' commission in Matthew 28:19–20:

> **Go therefore and make disciples of all nations, baptizing them in the name of the Father and of the Son and of the Holy Spirit, teaching them to observe all that I have commanded you.**

The person would then become a *catechumen*, which means one being educated. The term is used to describe the newly converted who is preparing for Baptism. It is in this stage that the person is taught the Christian faith, which is important particularly for adults. People were either coming from Judaism or from pagan philosophy and needed to rightly understand what Jesus taught. The time period of teaching varied depending on the situation and background of the person. During this stage, the person was considered an "enlightened one." If they were to die in that state, they would have been considered a believer because, by faith, they were trusting in God's Good News of His Son, Jesus. Yet because these adults were coming from one faith to another, instruction preceded Baptism as the norm. It's also important to note that the catechumen was not allowed to participate in the Lord's Supper, commonly called the Eucharist, at this stage. This would only take place after Baptism, the birth through the water into the church. However, the most natural way to enter the church was as an infant. Yes, through infant Baptism. God has always prioritized expanding His people starting at infancy—in the old covenant (circumcision) and the new covenant (Baptism). More on this later.

The church father Tertullian speaks of the prebaptismal stage this way in his work *On Repentance*, written around AD 198–200:

> **That *baptismal* washing is a sealing of faith, which faith is begun and is commended by the faith of repentance. We are not washed *in order that* we *may* cease sinning, but *because* we *have* ceased, since in *heart* we have *been* bathed already. For the *first* baptism of a learner is *this*, a perfect fear; thenceforward, in so far as you have understanding of the Lord faith *is* sound, the conscience having once for all embraced repentance.**[8]

It's important to notice how Baptism was considered early on as a "sealing of faith."

What I can appreciate about the ancient church's priority to train and form persons before Baptism was the seriousness with which they took the Christian life and the Sacraments. They were trained well so they could, if needed, catechize another.

This stands in contrast to an unfortunate trend in current

8 Tertullian, *On Repentance*, chapter 6 (*ANF* 3:662). Emphasis in original.

Christian culture in which many believers barely know what Christianity is or what the church teaches on foundational matters of the faith. This certainly contributes to why some have departed from the faith because of random YouTube theologians who make outlandish claims about Christianity and win over the vulnerable. In a lot of cases, churches focus more on experience over teaching, personal relationship above creeds, personal growth over being grounded in truth, intense praise over Christian formation.

The Christian life is about Jesus. It is about serving others as unto Jesus in the many ways God has designed you to serve. Loving others as we have been freely loved by Jesus. Growing more in our identity as the baptized into Christ Jesus. But we are not isolated, thinking only about ourselves. Baptism, as understood by the apostolic and church fathers, is all about identity in Christ Jesus and the community of the saints, that is to say, the church. The Lord's Supper is a communal meal whereby we are all united in our Lord and to one another. This is why we should not catch our cues from pop culture or pop-Christian culture, serving self over anything else or remaining isolated from others.

This isn't to say we should remain aloof to what is going on in the world. Nor is it to say we should not make efforts to stay plugged in to contemporary ways of communicating, engaging, entertaining, or educating. We should. We do right to consider how we can take neutral things in the world and yield them to the causes of Christ in the culture. Nevertheless, these things should be coupled with ancient creeds and confessions of the Christian faith in mind, guarding us and providing barriers and even context for what we say and how we demonstrate it to the surrounding society.

For example, I am a rap artist. Rap music, though more innocent in its origins, eventually became dominated by and known for violence and disrespect to women and authority. One could make the case that it should therefore be off-limits to Christians as a means to carry the precious pearl that is the Gospel. Although that argument is understandable, it is incomplete. Music can house any message placed in it, so it is well within biblical reasoning to take the pure format of rhythm and poetry and accompany it with Christ-centered lyrics, all for Christ's sake.

This is certainly how the some of the early church fathers used and thought of philosophy. Some figures sought to take the good from philosophy, if it existed, and yield it to the lordship of Jesus, the Christ. You will discover several of these people in this book. But for now, let's consider Justin Martyr on the matter. What you're about to read further demonstrates that Christians do right to identify things in the surrounding culture that we can tap into and use to connect with people and to meet them where they are with the goal of connecting them with Jesus for the forgiveness of sins and the life that flows from that forgiveness.

Since Justin Martyr studied philosophy and saw good in it, he thought it safe to preserve the good and helpful things about it for the sake of pointing people to their Savior, to the one who could rescue them from the dread and darkness of this life. He states in his *Second Apology*,

> **For whatever either lawgivers or philosophers uttered well, they elaborated by finding and contemplating some part of the Word. But since they did not know the whole of the Word, which is Christ, they often**

contradicted themselves.[9]

> Whatever things were rightly said among all men, are the property of us Christians. For next to God, we worship and love the Word who is from the unbegotten and ineffable God, since also He became man for our sakes, that becoming a partaker of our sufferings, He might also bring us healing. For all the writers were able to see realities darkly through the sowing of the implanted word that was in them. For the seed and imitation imparted according to capacity is one thing, and quite another is the thing itself, of which there is the participation and imitation according to the grace which is from Him.[10]

This statement expresses well that good, beautiful, and true things, wherever they are, should be preserved and valued as good. It also expresses that there is a neutrality to good things, capable of being coupled with clearer presentations of Jesus, our Lord, for the sake of serving others. Again, the Martyr says, "Whatever things were rightly said among all men, are the property of us Christians." Genius! I appreciate the assumption of origin. Justin assumes that God is the author. He is the originator who gives good gifts for us to use. It is unfortunate when good gifts are grasped by the wrong grip and used in the hands of evil men and women. It is the hands they are placed in that corrupts them. Otherwise, they can be used for good.

In the next statement that stands out to me, Justin highlights that there is an observability of the truth that is impossible to miss.

9 Justin Martyr, *The Second Apology of Justin*, chapter 10 (*ANF* 1:191).

10 *The Second Apology of Justin*, chapter 13 (*ANF* 1:193).

Because of sin, our sight is impaired and we can't fully observe what is right before us or trace where the truth leads: "For all the writers were able to see realities darkly through the sowing of the implanted word [logos] that was in them." Justin the Martyr believes that logos, associated with truth and reason among different philosophies, always points to Jesus, the ultimate Logos, the true Word and display of God on earth.

Justin recognizes Jesus as the Word, the full expression of what was known in part in times past, drawing on John 1:14–15:

> **And the Word became flesh and dwelt among us, and we have seen His glory, glory as of the only Son from the Father, full of grace and truth. (John bore witness about Him, and cried out, "This was He of whom I said, 'He who comes after me ranks before me, because He was before me.'")**

Justin confesses that Jesus is the sum total of the truth and wisdom humans have been grasping at for ages. Jesus is indeed the God-man, the one who holds all things together and heals the world of its brokenness. The things thinkers have been trying to work out, resolve, and reconcile for years, Jesus fixes in His personhood. He brings wholeness and restoration, and makes sense out of everything that perplexes us. He solves all the mysteries and perfectly counsels us back to soundness. He places us back in order with one another and the universe around us.

Another brother in the Lord who shared a similar sentiment is Clement of Alexandria, born around AD 150. In his writing *The Stromata, or Miscellanies*, he describes the way he views the intersection between philosophy and Christian theology, demonstrating that the church should use aspects of the wider society wherever we can to bring to bear the message of forgiveness founded in Christ Jesus:

> **Accordingly, before the advent of the Lord, philosophy was necessary to the Greeks for righteousness. And now it becomes conducive to piety; being a kind of preparatory training to those who attain to faith through demonstration. "For thy foot," it is said, "will not stumble, if thou refer what is good, whether belonging to the Greeks or to us, to Providence." For God is the cause of all good things; but of some primarily, as of the Old and the New Testament; and of others by consequence, as philosophy. Perchance, too, philosophy was given to the Greeks directly and primarily, till the Lord should call the Greeks. For this was a schoolmaster to bring "the Hellenic mind," as the law, the Hebrews, "to Christ." Philosophy, therefore, was a preparation, paving the way for him who is perfected in Christ.**[11]

By now you get my point. The church has always been apt to utilize what she could from the surrounding culture to make the message of the cross easier to process and digest. What we should not do is haphazardly form new Christians into people who think only about their personal relationship with Jesus or their own spiritual growth or their own walk with God. We should listen to the concepts and ideas around us to learn what terms people think and speak in so we can better convey the infinitely relevant message to

11 Clement of Alexandria, *The Stromata, or Miscellanies*, Book 1, chapter 5 (*ANF* 2:305).

needy sinners searching for identity and purpose.

We invite them into a community of people who are also sinners and sufferers but who have been reoriented by Christ Jesus. A gathering of individuals who have their own trauma, anxiety, fears, and mental health concerns but are resting in Jesus, who began our healing at our Baptism. A group whose souls are constantly stilled at the Lord's Supper, where we receive Christ's body and blood in the bread and wine. Persons who depend on one another and live in community, sharing one another's burdens.

By faith, as a sinner comes to recognize these things, they pursue reconciliation with this God of all creation, who reveals Himself in the person and work of Jesus, thus leading to inquiry, catechesis, and eventually Baptism as we mentioned above. During the early years of the church, bishops would often perform an exorcism to rid the person of demonic possession to break the power of the devil over their life. This was taken seriously due to citizens' regular participation in idol worship. They sought to destroy the demonic grip demons held over the person readying for Baptism. Yet, the bishops knew that ultimately, Baptism crushes the serpent's power as it delivers what Jesus won on the cross: our freedom from Satan and his grip on the human will.

New Christians were also warned to avoid those pagan temples so as to protect and guard the other members of the church. There was always a community goal for the early church. They thought much about being a unit uniquely joined together in Christ Jesus—not a mere metaphor to mean something like "Hey, look out for one another" but a true embrace of the mysterious unity believers share, joined in Christ.

After the exorcism was performed, the catechumen would publicly proclaim their faith in the Lord and denounce idol worship in every way as well as denounce Satan himself. Then the person would be baptized in the name of the Father, the Son, and the Holy Spirit. This would be followed by the declaration that the church was the house of the triune God, where the grace of forgiveness and life everlasting is communicated, delivered, and sustained.[12] This is such a beautiful component that I wish would be emphasized more in contemporary times.

We live in a time when the community aspect of the church is seen as an option. Life in community with fellow believers is seen as unnecessary, especially if you've been hurt by the church somehow. We sometimes downplay that the church is the body of our dear Lord Jesus, an organism He established and sustains with His own body and blood at the Lord's Supper and by the Holy Spirit and His Word. Beautiful!

From this point, the newly baptized would finally be permitted to partake in the Eucharist, a thing kept secret and distant from the catechumen earlier on in the process. Wow! What a fascinating process, capturing the sacred nature of the church and her rites established by Jesus, aiming to uphold the mystery of salvation delivered by means. Ultimately, this demonstrates that God is the one who does the work of salvation. He is the one who supernaturally unites Himself to earthly elements, by His Spirit, for the sake of conveying forgiveness, unity, and identity. It is clear that the early church attributed more to the Sacraments than empty symbolism that simply represents past accomplishments by Jesus.

12 See Angelo Di Berardino, *Ancient Christianity: The Development of Its Institutions and Practices* (ICCS Press, 2023).

CHAPTER 4

BAPTISM ACCORDING TO THE EARLY CHURCH

In years past, in my mind, the timeline of Christian history went something like this: the Bible days, Martin Luther, John Calvin, Billy Graham, my grandmother, then us. I would have never imagined there were tons of personalities throughout the ages that contributed to how we "do" Christianity today. Loads of debates set the context for how we talk about our faith. Plenty of meetings among Christians established creeds or summarized statements that define what Christianity is and how it ought to be understood. Those things were all new to me.

I recall hearing for the first time that the earliest of saints thought differently than I did about Baptism and the Lord's Supper. They talked about these Christian rites as activities that accomplish something spiritual, not as things we do to signal to God and others that we take our faith seriously. In fact, Ignatius of Antioch refers to the Lord's Supper as "the medicine of immortality, and the antidote to prevent us from dying."[13] Wow! That's a bold statement and one that can make the average Christian uncomfortable or even suspicious if they are not familiar with the history of the Holy Spirit's teachings.

I can definitely understand this hesitation. Having been coached from infancy onward to understand the Sacraments as outward signs of an inward change or a time to reflect on what Jesus did for us, I had no possible way to reconcile the Sacraments with our salvation and forgiveness. If someone said, "Baptism, which corresponds

13 *Epistle of Ignatius to the Ephesians*, chapter 20 (*ANF* 1:58).

to this, now saves you" (1 Peter 3:21), I felt forced to reject it. If Baptism is me using my physical limbs to walk forward to the baptismal pool after having decided in my heart to submit to Jesus, then how can that action possibly save me? A thing I did for myself, saving me? If the pastor is the one dunking me in the water and bringing me back up after having spoken Jesus' words over me, how can the pastor's actions be a part of saving me? The pastor has no special power to save. Therefore, Baptism cannot save because we are not saved by our works. Correct, we are not saved by our works. The question to ask is this: "Whose work is it?"

I recall being a kid at my Baptism. It was in West St. Louis, Missouri, at an African Methodist Episcopal church named Wayman Temple. I was probably around five years old, walking up the stairs in preparation to be robed. I was a bit nervous. Yet I knew I was doing something good, so that kept me calm. As I stood in line ready for my turn to approach the pastor, I glanced at the members in the pews and saw how happy everyone was for me. I came forward near the water, and the pastor began to speak to me through the microphone. He uttered some encouraging words, spoke the words of the Great Commission over me, and proceeded to dip me in the water and to quickly bring me up again. It was done. I was baptized. Life went on.

At age 16, after a near-death experience and the loss of my dear grandmother, I was finally ready to take my faith more seriously than I ever had before. I was invited to a Full Gospel Baptist church, where I would hear an appeal to give my life to Jesus. They called it an "altar call," and it went on for nearly forty minutes after the sermon was done. The choir leader sang a song that went something like this: "So come. You who are weary and heavy ladened. So come! Come on! To Christ." While the choir was singing, people were crying, wailing even. Others were swaying in place with their hands raised high and their eyes closed tightly. People were making a beeline to the altar and bowing on their knees there. Emotions were high. The mood was urgent and intense. The pastor paced about in front of the pulpit, urging visitors to step out into the aisle as an expression of faith toward God, to be courageous and publicly declare their faith in Jesus. Give Him your life today!

As I sat observing the room, I, too, was compelled to "give my life to Jesus." I slowly got up from my seat and moved out into the aisle and nervously walked forward. Cheers began to erupt. People were shouting and thanking God as I took step after step toward the line of elders manning the altar. The next step was to disclose your reason for coming forth to one of the leaders. I told the guy I wanted to give my life to the Lord. He began to share a bit more with me about what that meant. Then he started to pray fervently for me, that God would save me. That Jesus would "come into my heart." He invited me to make Jesus my personal Lord and Savior.

Eventually, they led you to the back of the church building to get your name, phone number, and address to follow up with you. I obliged. As time progressed, I found myself there for five years. I was never asked about Baptism. No one inquired if I was baptized before. It simply never came up.

Though I learned great things about our Lord, established lifelong friendships with many, and was taught foundational things about the Christian faith, my journey led me to Calvinism after about five years. I parted ways with the Pentecostal Baptist blend that is Full Gospel.

While in Bible college at a Reformed Baptist school, I was seeking to find a church home, as we say. I looked for a community of Christians to commit to and grow with. Eventually, I found that place. Expressing my desire to become a member, I was encouraged to speak with one of the elders to discuss my conversion experience. I did just that. I scheduled some time to work through the validity of my Christian conversion with the leaders.

We met in the pastor's office. Two elders accompanied us for the meeting. I sat across from them, and after a friendly greeting, they began to ask me about the nature of my "coming to Jesus" moment.

"Tell us a bit about your story," one elder said.

I briefly described my childhood and the ways the Christian faith informed my earlier days. Going to church. Reading my Bible. Even sharing the Word of God with my childhood friends. I conveyed the highlight reel of my Christian influence even as a young child in hopes that the two gentlemen would hear and know that my newfound appreciation of the faith was not a fluke but one that had deep roots and meaning tied to it.

As they sat across from me listening, I got the feeling that my childhood stories were falling flat, or at least not offering them the satisfaction of what they were seeking to hear. I knew it was time to switch gears. Quickly. I shifted the focus to how I had strayed from Christian morality in some ways. I shared moments of compromise and poor judgment on my part. I conjured up episodes of my life that did not show me in the best light, eventually leading me to despair and desperation, desperate for the things of God that my blessed grandmother had handed down to me.

Ahh, now we were getting somewhere! The two gentlemen perked up. The monologue began taking on the form of a "conversion story." Finally, I was sounding like a person who had gone through the darkness and found the "marvelous light!" As I brought the experiences to a turning point, I could sense the elders were hearing familiar language. The "uuumms" and "amens" were picking up. The smiles were forming on their faces.

From this point, they began to accept that I might be regenerated, that God had done a miracle in my life through His Holy Spirit. The next question they asked me was if I had been baptized or not.

"Yes, but it's tricky."

"How so?" one elder asked.

"At around five years old, I was baptized," I answered. "Yet I had my major lifestyle change after a car accident and the death of my grandmother."

The mood in the room changed as one elder asserted that the first experience at five years old should not be considered my Baptism but merely me getting wet. He explained that true Baptism must follow a true conversion experience. When one comes to the end of one's self and calls out to God for help. When one repents of their old ways and cries out to Jesus for mercy. And when one begins to bear fruit as proof that they had a genuine encounter with God. Then and only then should one be baptized. A Baptism after that type of dramatic shift can rightly be considered a biblical Baptism. Therefore, they insisted that I get baptized for what they considered to be the first time.

As a Reformed Baptist at the time, I obliged. I admit, I was a bit confused by it all because I knew my childhood walk with the Lord was true. I knew I bore fruit and was well aware of my Christian faith even as a young kid. I was not prepared to dismiss my experience outright, as it seemed the two elders had. I reserved some curiosity for another explanation but had nothing to support my suspicions at the time.

Nevertheless, I agreed to be baptized and to proclaim my faith publicly to honor and obey Christ through what they considered my first act of obedience. As I type and recall these moments, I can sense the anxiety I felt when I was in the room with those two elders that day. The pressure to feel sorry enough. The fear of not knowing if I was living holy enough. The fear of not being deemed worthy to be baptized. What a terrible departure from the gift and comfort that Baptism is and how it's been adored since the earliest days of the church.

Baptism being taught as optional or a work we do to signal to God and others how serious we are about Jesus is a grave deviation from what the early church taught. It was Tertullian who referred to believers as little fish and to Jesus as the big fish. He reminded his audience that one should abide in the water, the waters of Baptism, where the Holy Spirit descends into the water to work new birth by His power. Tertullian's work on Baptism, being one of the earliest contributions on the teaching, remains invaluable to the church and to the historic understanding of the Sacrament. This makes him and his treatise important and worth considering.

Tertullian of Carthage on Baptism

I first recall hearing of Tertullian while studying the doctrine of the Trinity extensively years ago. I was in Bible college being confronted with the topic afresh. My grandmother had taught me to confess the biblical teaching of the Trinity as a kid, but I was not aware of its deep historicity or of the controversies concerning the technical nature of the term and teaching of the Trinity. I did not know of Tertullian's contribution to the concept. He is even credited with being the one to coin the term *Trinity* in reference to the Godhead, or the nature of our God, who is three in one. It wasn't until recent years that I also came into awareness of his contribution to the understanding of Baptism.

If you grew up exclusively influenced by contemporary Christian thought like I did, you're probably wondering who in the church history is Tertullian in the first place. Good question! Tertullian is a figure from the third century. His lifetime has been dated from AD 160 to circa 230. It is interesting to note that he is African, specifically North African, and from a place called Carthage. Carthage was under the rule of the Romans at the time, which explains his extensive use and understanding of Latin.

Much more can be said related to his large contribution to Christian literature and his defense of the Christian faith, particularly against Gnosticism and other early heresies that posed a threat to biblical fidelity. For our purposes now, let's consider what we learn from his writings and thoughts connected to Baptism and the way third-century Roman Africa would have understood it. I guarantee you it is nothing like what most of us understand or think about when we hear the word *Baptism* or its meaning.

In one of the earliest treatises we have on Baptism, you can see how Baptism was viewed, how it offered comfort and assurance to consciences. I find this to be worth exploring. In our time, we struggle to see how Baptism should be a part of that conversation. When a person is consumed by fear or anxiety, their Baptism might be the last place they look. Baptism would seem like the worst topic to bring up when a family is grieving the loss of a Christian loved one. If a sermon were to mention Baptism or a pastor interjected its benefits into the conversation, the person may be confused and conclude that the pastor was disconnected from reality, that he had no relevant words of encouragement befitting the occasion.

We would prefer a catchy quote from social media that the algorithm included at just the right time to draw comfort. It would feel like an on-time word that God wanted us to hear. Typically, as humans, we love seemingly mystical coincidences like that. We would covet a prophetic word answering all our inquiries related to the future and present solutions for our grief. After all, what would Baptism have to say about the things we value? The pain, disappointment, and rejection you experience after a breakup? Healing from childhood trauma whose effects linger into our adulthood? Provision for our debt and payments for our bills? Advancement in our career fields? Social and political unrest? Suffering, disease, death, and martyrdom from persecution? False teaching? Surely Baptism is completely unrelated, useless, and irrelevant concerning these things, right? Wrong!

This is the unfortunate sentiment shared by many contemporary Christians. I've witnessed the utter disdain many harbor when Baptism is brought up in the abovementioned context from those who hold to the newly invented symbolic or metaphoric view. Nevertheless, this was not the case for Tertullian. In fact, this is how he starts off his treatise on Baptism: "Happy is our sacrament of water, in that, by washing away the sins of our early blindness, we are set free *and admitted* into eternal life!"[14] Sheesh! These are powerful words! Bold statements made about Baptism. Most importantly, biblical ones.

Life in this broken world is messy. The biggest mess of them all is the messiness of sin. Sin has corrupted our world and left it under a curse. Jesus, out of love, prioritized the handling of the biggest disorder of them all. He decided to defeat sin and death by taking on the punishment, the punishment that we deserve. He did

14 Tertullian, *On Baptism*, chapter 1 (*ANF* 3:669).

this for all humans without exception. Jesus paid for the sins of all. This is good news!

How does an individual access this truth, which is universal, for themselves particularly? How does someone apply and make use of the forgiveness that is theirs and has been won by Jesus during His earthly ministry? In other words, how does one apply to the self what Jesus earned on the cross? The Bible answers this question by telling us to be baptized for the forgiveness of sins (Acts 2:38).

The Bible tells us that to be baptized is to respond in faith alone to God's Word. To trust in God's Word alone. To receive the forgiveness of sins provided by Christ alone in the waters of Baptism. Water joined with His Word, accompanied by His Holy Spirit, so that you may be comforted and know the assurance of salvation on a personal level.

All this is delivered to each individual person as we are "watermarked" in our Baptism. It is a tangible touchpoint, a physical experience that we can recall and not question. It is more trustworthy than our feelings. Tertullian understood this and allowed it to echo from Scripture and then to ring throughout his own teachings concerning Baptism and its benefits.

Cyprian of Carthage on Baptism

In 2004, my first album dropped. It was self-titled. Up to that point, I was a local artist composing Christian rap songs from my parents' basement. I used to sit in an old-school student desk, studying the Bible and writing rap songs. (I wonder where my parents got that desk from? Maybe some thrift shop? I miss that desk.) Anyway, it was the spot where I'd reside and craft many theological discourses over beats.

By 2004, I was a convinced five-point Calvinist. I held to each point in the acronym *TULIP*. The *T* stands for total depravity. The *U* stands for unconditional election. The *L* is for limited atonement. The *I* is for irresistible grace. The *P* stands for perseverance of the saints, or the preservation of the saints. As I was learning to defend the TULIP, I was also learning to defend the Trinity. I thought, *What better way to clearly articulate and promote sound trinitarian teaching than through a song?*

The doctrine of the Trinity was near and dear to me. While I was in a moment of spiritual crisis, it was a study of the triune nature of our God that resuscitated my dying faith. I read a book by a popular Reformed Baptist apologist that utterly reinvigorated my soul. It was the beauty and wonder of the triune mystery that captivated my mind and emotions and kept me curious about God. It excited me to think about how each person in the Godhead worked in harmony to create the universe and to create faith in those dead in their sins. How God the Father, God the Son, and God the Holy Spirit, three in one, all harmoniously function to sustain faith in the Christian and see the person home safely. Beautiful!

In that study, I rediscovered the love of God, the one who is love (1 John 4:8), the mighty God, who is supreme over everything but uses His power not to crush but to comfort. Who in His vocation to the world decided to act on behalf of weak, anxious, fearful, and vulnerable people. Who within the triune counsel all agreed to send the Christ, Jesus the Savior, to save and seek out the lost. What an awe-inspiring study it was! It still fans the flames of gratitude in my life.

While working through the doctrine of the Trinity, I discovered groups and sects that disagreed with the historic trinitarian teaching of the church. One group in particular goes by the name of Oneness

Pentecostals or Apostolic Pentecostals. I learned that this community of people denied the Trinity. This movement popped on the scene around 1913 or 1914 and began to soil the Assemblies of God denomination with its false teachings on the matter.

Where are you going with this, Flame? I can hear you asking this. This is relevant to the topic because when they denied the Trinity, they then insisted that people must be baptized in Jesus' name only and not in the triune name of the Father, Son, and Holy Spirit. They altered the true nature of Baptism. They put themselves in a position over Jesus and His words and made themselves the final authority concerning Baptism. They claimed that if one was baptized in the name of Trinity (the Father, Son, and Holy Spirit), then it was not a valid Baptism, insisting that one be "rightly" baptized in Jesus' name only. They also taught that following Baptism, one must receive the Holy Spirit, as evidenced by the speaking of tongues, to be considered a genuine convert to the faith.

When I discovered this, I was moved to the core. My heart broke for those who had been deceived and had strayed from biblical teaching—lured into false teaching, which only and always adds burdens and a barrier to the freedom of the Gospel. Instantly, I was stirred to strike up a song on the subject. I began to develop a defense for the Trinity over rap tracks. I wanted to put to cadence correct confessions of the historic creeds of the church concerning the Godhead. So I did.

I titled the song "Real One." It is a tune offering a defense for the true nature of Jesus, the God-man, and defending the Trinity. I critiqued the Mormon understanding of God, the Jehovah's Witnesses, Christian Science, Islam, and Oneness Pentecostalism.

I must run this / It might get hostile / We don't want the Christ of Oneness Pentecostals / We want the incarnate Christ of the apostles / The pre-existent Son, the One of the Gospels / We want the real One!

These few lines ignited a fire that I did not see coming. Well, at least not from the direction I would have expected it. Little did I know, my hometown, St. Louis, Missouri, is the headquarters for the United Pentecostal Church International, the UPCI (technically, Weldon Spring, just outside of St. Louis). I had no idea that many people in my social circle and some close acquaintances were affiliated with them. Many were staunch and diehard members of the UPCI and stood on business about the movement.

When my debut album released, I visited a few bookstores for album signings to greet and engage the supporters of my music. In came a few familiar faces, but they did not look happy. I was concerned. One acquaintance asked if he could speak with me about something I said on the album.

"Definitely. What's up, bro?"

He began to explain that he was a Oneness Pentecostal and was deeply offended at the line "We don't want the Christ of Oneness Pentecostals." We shared a healthy dialogue during that moment and made plans to discuss it further on another occasion. We did just that. He was not won over and continued to deny the Trinity, unfortunately. It did not stop there. Many people from all over the United States began protesting to have my CD removed from all Christian bookstores. Groups gathered to toss my album in the trash in protest against my statement. Several college campus ministries began to host Bible studies to either affirm or deny the Trinity. I was invited to speak on several campuses and other venues to explain the line in the song and the thinking behind it. I accepted all those invitations and was more than happy to speak on the topic.

One of my main arguments was related to Baptism. Jesus clearly teaches that Baptism should be administered invoking the triune name, in the name of the Father, the Son, and the Holy Spirit. That is the biblical way. The counterargument from the Oneness Pentecostals' deviated perspective uses Acts 2:38:

> **And Peter said to them, "Repent and be baptized every one of you in the name of Jesus Christ for the forgiveness of your sins, and you will receive the gift of the Holy Spirit."**

They feel that this passage teaches that persons must be baptized in Jesus' name only, that when the pastor dips the person in the water, they can only say the words "We baptize you in the name of Jesus."

They misunderstand what's being said here. Peter is communicating to his audience that Baptism into the Christian faith is on the grounds of what Jesus the Messiah has claimed and accomplished for humanity. Under the authority of Jesus and His revelation of reality, we comply and humble ourselves and confess that He is the way. Under no other effort or authority can a person be reconciled or made right with the God of the universe. This is made possible by Jesus.

It is through this person of the Trinity, Jesus alone, who has the credentials to make such a demand, that one can be brought into a state of forgiveness by Baptism. The letters *J-e-s-u-s* by themselves cannot save anyone. The same goes for the letters *Y-e-s-h-u-a*. If my little cousin's name is Jesus, spelled *J-e-s-u-s*, that would not automatically give him the ability to forgive sins. The letters *J-e-s-u-s* are not inherently powerful. The power to forgive sins is because of who the incarnate (enfleshed) Son of God is. He is indeed God in flesh. That's why Peter told the crowd to be baptized under Jesus' authority as opposed to another's.

Peter's words in Acts 2:38 in no way contradict or conflict with Jesus' words in Matthew 28:19:

> **Go therefore and make disciples of all nations, baptizing them in the name of the Father and of the Son and of the Holy Spirit.**

Jesus established this holy rite of Baptism to bind together and place the baptized person into communion with the triune God of all creation. Notice Jesus uses the singular word *name* and not the plural *names*. This is because God is one. One God in three persons. We are not baptized into many names but into one name—the name of the Father, Son, and Holy Spirit. The Trinity.

Peter knew this. He was taught this firsthand by Jesus Himself. The words before the Great Commission read as follows (Matthew 26:16–17):

> **Now the eleven disciples went to Galilee, to the mountain to which Jesus had directed them. And when they saw Him they worshiped Him.**

Yes, the apostle Peter was one of the eleven at the mountain, hearing directly from Jesus these words. So when in Acts 2:38 he says to be baptized in Jesus' name, he is speaking confidently about the way of Christianity taught directly to him by Jesus on the mountain. He is insisting that all those hearing his sermon turn from heeding other voices and obey only the voice of Jesus, the way, the truth, and the life.

It follows that to be baptized in Jesus' name means to receive, by faith, the forgiveness of sins through Baptism in the name of the Father, the Son, and the Holy Spirit. By the power of Jesus' Word, the sinner is now made a saint and placed into relationship with the triune God through the water tied to Jesus' Word. That is what Baptism is. To go under the water in the name of *J-e-s-u-s*, who is not the Second Person of the Trinity, is not Baptism, according to Jesus. According to Scripture.

Cyprian of Carthage comes to mind, as he also dealt with splits among the saints that resulted in break-off sects threatening Scripture's instructions concerning the church and Holy Baptism in his day. Cyprian, a brother in the Lord, was born in the beginning of the third century. He, too, was from the North African city called Carthage. He became a believer at thirty-five years of age. That's when he was baptized into the faith.

It is interesting to note that our dear brother was arrested for his allegiance to Christ in AD 258. That arrest eventually led to his martyrdom by beheading. It all stemmed from a persecution that arose under the heavy hand of Emperor Valerian in 256. That persecution made its way to North Africa and met Cyprian, who refused to make a sacrifice to Emperor Valerian. His only response to the sentence of death was "Deo gratias!"—that is, "Thanks be to God!" He stripped off his own clothes, put on the blindfold, and stretched out his neck for the sword.

The unity of the church was important to Cyprian, including the preservation of such gifts as salvation by Baptism. He knew that it was through the church that God births children into His kingdom. Cyprian states, "She keeps us for God. She appoints the sons whom she has born for the kingdom."[15] The "she" is the church. Therefore, it is important that if anyone is seeking to be a part of God's kingdom, they should be born in the community of saints, who rally around the Word of God rightly understood, the nature of God rightly understood, and the Sacraments rightly understood.

Like me and my concern for those who were being taught to denounce or deny the Trinity, Cyprian contested similar things in his time. For him, if a person was "dipped" in a community of people who claimed to be Christians but taught false things about God, he could not vouch for their dipping. In an epistle, or letter, he wrote to a fellow bishop named Quintus concerning the baptism of heretics, he made some bold statements and took hard but important stances against false baptisms.

A heretic is a false teacher who uses Christian language but changes the meaning of the language and confuses people. Heretics distort the truths of God and hang around Christian circles in hopes of recruiting members to their way of thinking. They may be nice people. Many are caring and sacrificial. You may not be able to tell that they are deceiving individuals by the way they look or the way they act. This is why it is important to understand God's Word and the historic teachings of the church, to be equipped to stand against false teachings—ultimately, to live in the freedom of the Gospel and not the added burden of false doctrine. Salvation, as argued by Cyprian, is a reality born out of the unity of the church, the unity of a correct confession of biblical truths and leaders who teach rightly and rightly administer the Sacraments—in particular in this case, the Sacrament of Baptism.

Cyprian is clear about where salvation lies: within the church, where God delivers His gifts. A popular mantra attributed to the

15 *The Treatises of Cyprian*, Treatise 1, *On the Unity of the Church*, paragraph 6 (*ANF* 5:423).

North African is "He can no longer have God for his Father, who has not the Church for His mother."[16] So if a person goes under the water outside of the one true church, there is no peace. Again, Cyprian refers to the church as "holy Mother Church." It is safer to say there is no salvation outside of the church, meaning the universal gathering of believers all across the globe who confesses the creeds that unite us: the Nicene Creed, the Athanasian Creed, and the Apostles' Creed. Each one of these statements of faith affirms what the Bible teaches about what Christianity is at its core: Who God is and how we ought to understand His nature as a triune God. How we should think about salvation and what it means to be saved from sin. How God delivers His gifts through Baptism to bring poor sinners into His kingdom.

> **But if he who comes from the heretics has not previously been baptized in the Church, but comes as a stranger and entirely profane, he must be baptized, that he may become a sheep, because in the holy Church is the one water which makes sheep.**[17]

This is a wonderful confession that states clearly what Baptism is. It demonstrates how the early church understood Baptism. That it is a must. That it makes sheep. That there is one Baptism, or one water. That it happens in the holy church, not outside the church in any random community teaching "kind of" or pseudo-Christian ideas.

Baptism simply was not talked about as an outward expression or sign of an inward change. This early church father spoke of Baptism as a reality that makes sheep. In context, a sheep, in keeping with biblical imagery, is a follower of the Good Shepherd, Jesus, the

16 Cyprian, *On the Unity of the Church*, paragraph 6 (*ANF* 5:423).
17 *The Epistles of Cyprian*, Epistle 70, paragraph 2 (*ANF* 5:377).

Savior. How does one go from being considered "a stranger and entirely profane" to a sheep? By abandoning false teaching and, by faith, being baptized in the holy church.

No other washing or dipping offers salvation. There is only one Baptism. This is what Paul taught us in Ephesians 4:5–6: "One Lord, one faith, one baptism, one God and Father of all."

In this is much comfort. Much peace. A true stabilizing act of God that brings rest to the heart. This one Baptism is where God makes sheep and promises to guard them. To lead them throughout life. To make their way straight and to see them home safely. And when they stray, to call them back to safe pastures away from harm and danger. Cyprian refuses to yield this comfort to heretics.

I know many people who developed a troubled conscience and were "rebaptized" in Jesus' name only out of fear that they were now hell-bound because of being baptized in the triune name. That is unfortunate. Baptism is a gift from God. It is not a work we perform in Jesus' name only to get the prize of acceptance. Furthermore, it should be noted that the Oneness Pentecostal community also teaches that Baptism is simply an outward sign of an inward expression. They believe Baptism is purely your first act of obedience, signaling to God and others a genuine desire to change for Christ, only symbolizing a fresh start and newfound allegiance to God. This is odd because after all the fuss and formulaic emphasis, their version of the rite is not an actual means of grace.

Another person I know used to think he had to "get saved" every Sunday at the altar and that, after an accumulated amount of "backsliding," he needed to renew his Baptism. For him, Baptism marked the time he decided to take his faith more seriously. If he strayed from that seriousness in a way that he arbitrarily decided, then he determined the only way back to God's good graces was to show Him he was willing to be baptized again. A public display of commitment. An important proclamation to renew his "personal relationship" with God.

For these reasons and many others, quite a few Christians have gone under the water in the name of Baptism numerous times in different formats: christenings, sprinklings, full immersion; in the name of the Father, the Son, and the Holy Spirit, or in Jesus' name only. All in hopes of securing their place on God's good side. In hopes of finding comfort and assurance. Hoping that they have done what God requires to gain access to His heaven. They are missing out on the actual miracle that takes place in Baptism.

Augustine of Hippo on Baptism

When I first started to talk about how the church has always understood Baptism as a means of grace to deliver forgiveness, many people thought I made it up. Or worse, that I was teaching false doctrine. On January 24, 2020, I released a project titled *Extra Nos*, which is a Latin phrase that means "outside ourselves." The phrase helps us remember that we look to what Jesus accomplishes for us as opposed to our own merits.

This is the case for the new Christian, the mature Christian, and the seasoned Christian alike. We all must continue to look to Jesus and His righteousness, applied to us by faith continuously through His Word and Sacraments for justification. In the *Extra Nos* project, I sought to expose my audience to a clearer understanding of justification, one more historic than what had been presented in the Reformed Baptist understanding of justification.

In the short project, I did not expand extensively on the Sacraments, but I did show my hand and expose that there was more to come. In the song "Ordo Salutis," I tied Baptism, the Lord's Supper, and faith together in a way that would signal to my audience that there are other aspects to the conversation:

> *Faith is gift / I've been baptized / I meet Him at the altar in the bread and the wine / It's more than a sign / That's why it's emphasized / That since Christ died only faith justifies / Boy, faith is a gift.*

I made the same move, in brief, a second time in the song named "Used to Think":

> *If our faith justifies us / And God saved and baptized us / We set our gaze outside of us / Extra nos.*

I recall a portion of listeners being curious about what Baptism and the Lord's Supper have to do with salvation. They were taught Christianity the same way I was taught it, that Baptism and Communion are ritual activities that we do from time to time to reflect on what Jesus did a long time ago or to show the world that we are different. The notion that our justification is delivered to us in our Baptism is utter blasphemy to some. The assertion that forgiveness of sins is applied to us anew at the Lord's Supper is unfortunately understood as a mockery of the work Jesus accomplished on the cross. This is mostly because people think this idea is Roman Catholic, and we were taught to dismiss Rome from the conversation. Out goes healthy discussion about the Sacraments.

Knowing that the conversation about Baptism would take more time to unpack and also having been more deeply impacted by the historic understanding of the Lord's Supper at the time, I decided that my next project should be on the Eucharist. Exactly one year and five days from the EP *Extra Nos* taking my audience by storm, January 29, 2021, I unleashed *Christ for You*, an entire project on the Lord's Supper. Still no major points were made about baptismal regeneration in the music. The only line about Baptism comes from a song on the EP titled "Sounds Crazy":

> ***Told Peter come walk on the water / Plus He made wine out of water / Baptized us in the water.***

At that point, I had only made three public statements in song format about my better understanding of Baptism. One tied Baptism to faith and justification. The other two spoke of God baptizing. I don't think everyone caught the important nuance that is. Obviously, there are people who simply appreciated the cadence and the overall vibe of the song. Others heard it but mistakenly thought the language meant what they already believed about Baptism. Then there are more perceptive listeners who questioned the turn of phrase.

The questions began to arise. *What do you mean God baptized us? What do you mean Jesus baptized us in the water? Why did you say "faith is a gift / I've been baptized" as if Baptism has something to do with being saved? What about the thief on the cross?* And so on. As I started to engage many of these questions in comment sections on social media, I realized it was now time to unpack the big topic of Baptism in music format.

I took my time to carefully craft an EP on the matter. April 29, 2022—one year and three months later—I would unleash *Word and Water* to the masses. Finally, I had drawn a line in the sand surrounding the subject of Baptism, defending the historic view of

Baptism as a work of God and not a work we perform, articulating the ancient understanding of Baptism as preserved through confessional Lutheran thought.

"Heresy! Heresy!" some proclaimed.

"Flame is an apostate! He has left Christianity!" others shouted.

If I had to narrow it down to the core gripe listeners were having, it would be the struggle to understand how I could proclaim justification by faith alone and at the same time teach baptismal regeneration—indeed, that Baptism saves (1 Peter 3:20–21). For them, that was a major contradiction, two things that cannot both be true.

An interesting thing to note is the particular mood or attitude of that time period—the context in which *Word and Water* was released, one that lingers today even as I type. During that time, it became a cultural norm to speak in the language of "deconstruction." People wanted to strip Christianity down to its bare roots to assess what it truly is and is not. A great many individuals were questioning their personal faith in the Bible, growing in skepticism surrounding Christianity and its origins altogether, asking if colonization is the cause of Christianity. They wondered if "the white man" invented it to control the masses of people.

Succumbing to much of this madness, many began overthrowing the Christian narrative and departing from the faith. Among the many who held fast to their faith, some also developed a more critical disposition toward "new ideas." I recall someone telling me that they didn't want to believe anything attached to a person. What they meant was a set of teachings tied to a person and/or an "ism," like Calvinism (John Calvin), Arminianism (Jacobus Arminius), Lutheranism (Martin Luther), or even patristics (the church fathers). They developed an inherent distrust of anything that seemed to be promoting a person or a systematic way of doing theology. Due to the timing of my release, unfortunately, a good number of those people swept what I was presenting into the category of a "new idea" or into an "ism," thus making it easier to dismiss or to not even engage.

The task for me became to prove that what I was arguing for was not an "ism" or a thing focused on propping up a person as special. It is not some new concept or the presentation of a new sect. No! Not a new spin-off concept rooted in Christian verbiage but diverted from historic Christian teachings and now camped out around churchgoers to trick them into our little group. No!

Nothing like Hebrew Israelites claiming to have some hidden insights that will enlighten you and earn you more favor with God and advancements in the world. No! Not an ethnocentric emphasis of the faith that promises change if you would only learn who you are as God's special race of people and understand the Bible our way. Not at all! The truths that I am speaking of go back to the earliest days of the church. Truths that rang true from a broad spectrum of believers from all over the known world claiming to be followers of the triune God of the Christian faith.

These are teachings that men and women were martyred for, sacramental teachings that the church guarded with their minds and their might from the East to the West. True pastors met regularly and communicated about, especially, matters of schism, false doctrine, and division. They discussed sound teachings that were assumed and universally agreed on even if customs differed slightly from place to place or from century to century.

The historic understanding of the church and her early confessions became an important talking point for me to stress. I felt the burden of helping people understand that their take on the Sacrament of Baptism—and the Lord's Supper—was the newest one, one that is foreign to our ancient heritage. One that was formed as a response to conflict and proved to be a savvy political play, an attempt to rid Rome of her power. More on that when we discuss Baptism during the time of the Reformation.

A key figure who is helpful to discuss, who is known even among many generic American Christian groups, is Augustine of Hippo. His is one of those names that shows up in quite a few different camps. People find quotes from him and post them on social media. They love his book *Confessions*, yet a great number of Christians don't know much about him, specifically about his biblical teaching on Baptism.

Augustine of Hippo was another African pastor and theologian from the northern region. He was born in AD 354 to his Christian mother, Monica. He was well educated and is regarded as one of the most influential minds that shaped Western Church thought. His impact on the church at large is of the highest significance. Because of his own writings, he is known for more than just his theological prowess. He is also known for being a "wild boy" at one stage of his life. He confessed to having a child outside of marriage with a woman he was drawn to. Augustine is very much like us all—a sinner and a saint.

Notably, his mom prayed fervently for him, that God would rescue him from the grips of sin and Satan. God did just that. The North African scholar would eventually come under the influence of an older scholar and pastor: Ambrose, Archbishop of Milan. Ambrose's teachings and rhetoric impressed Augustine and challenged his ways of thinking about reality and the world around him.

Eventually, Augustine became a student of Ambrose and was baptized under his auspice. In due time, this led to Augustine's ordination as a priest, which then blossomed into his bishopric. As a bishop, he used a great deal of his talent writing about the Bible and the church. His contribution in this regard cannot be understated. He went to bat for the truth of God among a few significant controversies. For our considerations here, let's examine what he had to say related to Baptism and its nature related to the church and doctrine.

There are many layers to the situation between Augustine and the group of Christians known as the Donatists. We will mostly examine Augustine's view of Baptism in relation to his disagreements with the Donatists. This is to further undergird how the early church understood the rite of Baptism differently than it is understood today in many Christian camps.

The Donatists were a collection of North African Christians who splintered into their own group after major persecution broke out. The group got its name from their leader, Donatus of Casae Nigrae. The Roman Emperor Diocletian demanded that citizens pledge their allegiance to him by performing religious rituals. Obviously, this was a problem for Christians because we devote all our spiritual worship, allegiance, and acknowledgment of ultimate lordship to the triune God alone. This meant nothing to Diocletian.

Other requirements for Christians were to turn over sacred writings, Scriptures, and Christian trinkets, to submit them to authorities or be punished or executed. Under such demands, as one can imagine, many succumbed to the pressure and complied with Diocletian's orders, handing over precious material to preserve their lives and livelihoods. The Christians who did became labeled as traitors.

The Donatists saw that type of weakness or compromise as idolatry. They concluded that those persons had punted the faith and fallen from grace. If a pastor or bishop was numbered among the traitors, the Donatists taught that they could no long administer the Sacraments or ordain other bishops and that, consequently, they had left the church and her graces. They took this hard stand against the church in North Africa and elsewhere, and they claimed to be the one and only pure church, the true church of Scripture.

If a person wanted to return to the church and be a part of the community, the Donatists demanded that they get rebaptized. They were viewed as having fallen from the grace of God given in Baptism. If a person was baptized by a bishop who became a "traitor," they, too, needed to be rebaptized because the Donatists saw the first Baptism as invalid. Even if a person left the Catholic Church and sought membership among the Donatists, their Baptism was not accepted because the Donatists saw the Catholic Church as not having the ability to baptize in truth because they accepted such traitors in their midst.

Augustine, on the other hand, did not place the grace given in Baptism in the hands of the one administering it but in God alone. He was not willing to hand that power and impact over to the baptizer. Arguing from Scripture, he defended the Sacrament's efficacy by rooting it in Jesus' spiritual power and not the spiritual aptitude of the bishop performing the rite or in the bishop's moral performance. Baptism remains effective because Jesus established it. It is His idea, a reality that cannot be tainted by anything.

Even if a person was baptized in the Donatist movement, a movement Augustine viewed as a schism, he did not consider the Baptism invalid. This is because, even though the Baptism was performed outside of the Catholic Church, he acknowledged that the power rested in the nature of Baptism provided by Jesus. Though he desired the Donatists to unite with the church and to dispel their splinter group, he did not dismiss that God was active, baptizing even among their schism.

In an effort to describe the power of Baptism resting in Christ and not in the minister, the Bishop of Hippo says this:

> **If the minister is righteous, I reckon him with Paul, I reckon him with Peter; with those I reckon righteous ministers: because, in truth, righteous ministers seek not their own glory; for they are ministers, they do not wish to be thought judges, they abhor that one should place his hope on them; therefore, I reckon the righteous minister with Paul.**[18]

Augustine specifically relates this passage to Baptism, as the apostle Paul does. He assures his audience that the one who makes the increase or delivers the results is God Himself, not the one administering the rite. He then shifts to discuss the character of the minister who is after self-glorification:

> **But he who is a proud minister is reckoned with the devil; but the gift of Christ is not contaminated, which flows through him pure, which passes through him liquid, and comes to the fertile earth. Suppose that he is stony, that he cannot from water rear fruit; even through the stony channel the water passes, the**

18 Augustine, *Lectures or Tractates on the Gospel According to St. John*, Tractate 5, chapter 1.33, paragraph 15 (*NPNF1* 7:37).

water passes to the garden beds; in the stony channel it causes nothing to grow, but nevertheless it brings much fruit to the gardens.[19]

Plainly put, the salvific gift delivered in Baptism is not contaminated by the person performing the rite. The person is a tool, a vessel, whereby God accomplishes His ends. God will make sure the receiver gets the blessings without hindrance.

For the spiritual virtue of the sacrament is like the light: both by those who are to be enlightened is it received pure, and if it passes through the impure it is not stained. Let the ministers be by all means righteous, and seek not their own glory, but His glory whose ministers they are.[20]

Yes, Augustine encourages the ministers to be undefiled, to honor their vocation, to not haphazardly function in their role. Nevertheless, he makes it clear that on God's behalf, God will be sure to love His own no matter what, using both the just minister and the evil minister to baptize—indeed, to save. Ultimately, the Bishop of Hippo understands that Baptism is God's work. God is the active one. Therefore, Augustine admonishes the proud minister: "Jesus, therefore, is still baptizing; and so long as we continue to be baptized, Jesus baptizeth."[21]

Augustine makes a compelling argument based on John 4:1–2, which says,

Now when Jesus learned that the Pharisees had

19 Augustine, *Lectures* 5.1.33.15 (*NPNF1* 7:37).

20 Augustine, *Lectures* 5.1.33.15 (*NPNF1* 7:37).

21 Augustine, *Lectures*, Tractate 15, chapter 4.1–42, paragraph 3 (*NPNF1* 7:100).

> **heard that Jesus was making and baptizing more disciples than John (although Jesus Himself did not baptize, but only His disciples).**

This text reminds us that ultimately Jesus gets the credit for baptizing. Yet He uses sinful people to do so. Unworthy men who doubt Him, who betray Him, who compete for positions of prominence and seek to be exalted, who abandon Him, who sell Him out for money. Nevertheless, He gets the credit for the good that He works through such earthly vessels. He remains faithful and does not withhold the good just because the carrier of the good thing is tainted. No, He preserves His gifts in their purest form for the sake of the world!

The essence of the debate itself exposes the church's assumption: that Baptism saves. That Baptism is a means of grace that brings one into Christ Jesus. That Baptism places one in the Body of Christ, the church. The fact that Augustine is debating with the Donatists about where the power in Baptism resides is telling. Does Baptism unite one with Christ Jesus and His church by the power of the Spirit flowing through the pastor based on the pastor's upright life? Or does Baptism stand on its own, rooted in the very nature of it being instituted by Jesus Himself, who saves through it? Consider this statement from Augustine:

> **When baptism is given in the words of the gospel, however great be the perverseness of understanding on the part either of him through whom, or of him to whom it is given, the sacrament itself is holy in itself on account of Him whose sacrament it is.**[22]

22 Augustine, *On Baptism, Against the Donatists*, Book 4, chapter 12 (*NPNF1* 4:455).

The bishop then goes on to further link salvation and Baptism together in keeping with Scripture and the teachings of the church:

> **And if any one, receiving it at the hands of a misguided man, yet does not receive the perversity of the minister, but only the holiness of the mystery, being closely bound to the unity of the Church in good faith and hope and charity, he receives remission of his sins.**[23]

How water tied to God's Word can deliver forgiveness is indeed a mystery. A holy mystery, Augustine calls it. One that we embrace by faith simply because Jesus established this truth with His Word. When Baptism is done in God's triune name according to Jesus' own command, the person will have an encounter with the grace of God. Whether they receive the benefits by faith is a different story.

On that matter, Augustine says,

> **But if the recipient himself be misguided, on the one hand, what is given is of no avail for the salvation of the misguided man; and yet, on the other hand, that which is received remains holy in the recipient, and is not renewed to him if he be brought to the right way.**[24]

In Baptism, Jesus is there to forgive sins. This much will always be true. If one is clinging to the promise of forgiveness with the faith of a mustard seed, yes, even the smallest amount of faith, they will be saved. Again, as Augustine states, "Being closely bound to the

23 Augustine, *On Baptism* 4.12 (*NPNF1* 4:455).
24 Augustine, *On Baptism* 4.12 (*NPNF1* 4:455).

unity of the Church in good faith and hope and charity, he receives remission of his sins." This is good news. Baptism is Gospel!

Irenaeus of Lyons on Baptism

One of the main struggles people have with the reality that God uses Baptism to deliver the forgiveness of sins won by Jesus on the cross for all and to give us His Holy Spirit is that they get stuck defending the bottom line while not being aware of a major blind spot. Christians are sure about the following:

1. They know salvation is the work of the Lord.
2. They know God gets the glory for our salvation, not us.
3. They know we are not saved by our works.
4. They know we are justified by faith alone.

These are bottom-line realities from which we should never budge, but people can get stuck trying to understand how Baptism can do what Peter says it does—save (1 Peter 3:20–21).

They have no path of understanding in their thinking or theology that can reconcile these seemingly contradictory statements. Therefore, they dismiss and oftentimes outright ignore or deny the plain meaning of a text that states Baptism washes away sins, such as Acts 22:16:

> **And now why do you wait? Rise and be baptized and wash away your sins, calling on His name.**

Because this *seemingly* conflicts with the bottom line and encroaches on the nonnegotiable truth that we are justified by faith alone, they begin a scavenger hunt through the Bible to prove we must *only* "repent and believe" to be saved. That by faith, apart from means, we are forgiven. They pit Scripture against Scripture in an effort to protect the bottom line.

They cannot track down how the Bible can mean both statements without contradicting itself. The Bible says we are justified by faith, and it says Baptism saves. Their solution to this is to cancel the Baptism passages, make the Baptism passages metaphorical, claim that Baptism is not with real water but is symbolic of leaving your old life for a new one in Christ, teach to "Spirit Baptism." And again they assert and restate the bottom line, justification by faith.

They toss around statements like "sola fide" or "justification by faith alone," removing them from their historic context, in which they were always coupled with baptismal regeneration and the mystical union of the Lord's Supper, all tied to God's Word of promise, based on and rooted in Christ alone—in Jesus' incarnation, sinless life, crucifixion, resurrection, and ascension. Never in conflict. Never.

To reveal the blind spot, those persons should prayerfully move slower through Scripture concerning Baptism and consider with it the history of the Holy Spirit's teaching to His church throughout the ages:

1. Baptism is God's work, not ours. God baptizes us. Yes, we use our limbs to walk forward to the baptismal pool or font. Yes, God uses the pastor or person to apply the water. Yes, there is real H_2O. Water. Nevertheless, it is God who does the verbs. He drowns the sinner and raises them to newness of life. Humans have zero power to do that.

2. Baptism is God's Word of forgiveness, comfort, and assurance wedded with real water.
3. God uses physical means to deliver the benefits of what Jesus earned on the cross for sinners: the forgiveness of sin. He can use the preached Word, the written Word, and the visible Word, Baptism, to save, and the Lord's Supper to forgive sin (Matthew 26:28).
4. This does not conflict with justification by faith alone. Why? Because by faith alone, one trusts in whatever God says. By faith alone, one receives from God what He says He delivers however He says He delivers it. If Jesus said it, we trust His Word. Even if it's difficult to wrap our minds around intellectually.
5. Baptism is nowhere spoken of, in all of Scripture, as a first act of obedience or as a symbol of salvation or as a follow-up to show the world that you're a Christian. So why trust those catchphrases as opposed to plain passages that actually say what Baptism does? "And Peter said to them, 'Repent and be baptized every one of you in the name of Jesus Christ for the forgiveness of your sins, and you will receive the gift of the Holy Spirit'" (Acts 2:38). Notice the word *for*. This is what repentance and Baptism is *for*.
6. The word *and* means "along with" or "also." Repentance (contrition and faith) and Baptism are

inherently tied together and should not be separated. It is God who gives us the power to experience contrition and faith (repentance). In Baptism, He applies the benefits of forgiveness. He repents us.

7. Don't fight to find the exception to the rule over against the teaching Jesus clearly states and emphasizes as His desired norm. This is done when people harp on whether you can get saved without Baptism. Why shift Jesus' focus and emphasis to another one? Why fight to show we don't need to be baptized to be saved? That's an arrogant agenda after knowing Jesus tied salvation and Baptism together: "Whoever believes and is baptized will be saved, but whoever does not believe will be condemned" (Mark 16:16). And "Jesus answered, 'Truly, truly, I say to you, unless one is born of water and the Spirit, he cannot enter the kingdom of God'" (John 3:5). In all of the New Testament, salvation and Baptism are joined. Always.

8. The Bible does *not* say the thief on the cross *wasn't* baptized. People assume and read that into the Bible. Holy writ does *not* say that. Even if he wasn't baptized, he received the same word of forgiveness and comfort Jesus gives in Baptism, that we are forgiven and will be with Him in paradise. Hallelujah!

9. We are the baptized. It is our identity. We

are ones watermarked by God in His triune name. Our daily walk is dying and being raised to newness of life (Romans 6:3–4).

10. Baptism is a sweet means of forgiveness, comfort, and assurance of salvation. A reality we can depend on beyond our feelings, affections, and performance. A means of grace. God's Word, indeed. The Gospel. Heaven coming down to earth. The work of God on our behalf using water joined to His sweet word of forgiveness.

One of the major root causes of contemporary Christianity's stumbling in this area is the false notion that true spirituality has to happen inside of us or apart from means. That it must be invisible or a deeply heartfelt experience, a personal one that just "feels real." If one claims that God uses normal physical things to deliver grace, it is assumed to be cheap or less impressive, a thing to doubt because a powerful God would seem more godlike if He did something entertaining or showy. We crave big flexes, especially from God. Something out of the ordinary. This is perhaps due to the influence of an ancient teaching called Gnosticism.

Gnosticism, at its core, was an effort to deal with the problem and reality of evil in the world, as well as to understand how finite or temporal and limited things can exist at the same time with endless and limitless things. In order to deal with such questions, an entire system of understanding was developed. Gnosticism is a loaded and layered school of thought that varies depending on which branch, which set of teachers were expanding on it, and which generation was leading it. Yet a few concepts seem to be consistent. One is that humans need saving from evil (which is true), and another is that salvation is accomplished by knowledge (which is not true). A final pillar in the Gnostic understanding of salvation is that physical matter is evil and off limits to any saving effort—and therefore something God should know better than to utilize in the drama of redemption.

This type of theology began to gain momentum and infiltrate biblical Christianity. It posed a threat to the many believers who came near its venomous claims. Early forms of it reared their ugly faces during New Testament times. The apostle John dealt with it in his epistles. Ultimately, it was the person and work of Christ Jesus Himself that came under attack by Gnosticism. Gnostics taught that Jesus could not possibly be the God-man, because God would have nothing to do with physicality—at least according to their teaching that flesh is evil. Therefore, the eternal Son of God would never assume human flesh in order to redeem humanity. Despite early teachings of John that refuted this, the following centuries really felt the brunt of Gnosticism.

This leads us to consider Irenaeus, an early church father who defended against this false teaching, which attacked the true nature of Christ, of salvation, and of God using physical means to save. Guess what Irenaeus discusses to defend truth claims concerning Christianity and salvation? Yep, you guessed it—Baptism! Before we get into that, though, let's learn a bit about our good brother.

Irenaeus lived around AD 130–200. An extremely interesting and important thing to know about him is that he was taught by Polycarp. Polycarp was taught by the apostle John, one of Jesus' closest followers. Wow! This is a fact that should not be taken lightly. It gives Irenaeus a level of credibility that at least demands one's serious consideration. It begs that we sit at his feet to gather as much as we can related to how the early church understood Christianity, salvation, and the Sacraments.

As a Greek man raised in a place called Smyrna, Irenaeus would have been exposed to Polycarp's bishopric and become one of Polycarp's students. Eventually, he became a pastor and practiced his vocation in Lyons, France. While Irenaeus was taking a trip to Rome carrying a letter from his bishop dealing with a false teaching about Jesus' nature, his bishop was martyred. Irenaeus was then made bishop in his place.

Most famously, Irenaeus is known for his writing *Against Heresies*, which refuted Gnostic thought. It is a relatively large body of work, aimed at dismantling the notion that Christianity and Gnosticism are compatible and ultimately at annihilating Gnosticism to render it powerless, to strip it out of Satan's hands as a weapon used to cut down the faith of many Christians.

He attacks Gnostic claims that there is a better way to practice the Christian faith. He does so by using the Bible and expounding on Scripture, proving to be a skilled theologian and scholar in defense of the faith. He also utilizes widely accepted teachings of the church and the church's traditions to combat this new idea being sold to the saints.

As I was being exposed to him and his passion for contending for the faith, I could not help but relate and be inspired by how he tied Baptism into his defense of the faith. In this, I was challenged. I would never have thought Baptism could fortify the faith against false teaching. It was a penetrating point and important to Irenaeus to simplify salvation for those succumbing to Gnosticism. To call them back to the ordinary way in which God chose to save, in contrast with the complicated and confusing religion of the Gnostics.

The pastor from Smyrna has this to say about the Gnostic system:

> **It happens that their tradition respecting *redemption* is invisible and incomprehensible, as being the mother of things which are incomprehensible and invisible; and on this account, since it is fluctuating, it is impossible simply and all at once to make known its nature, for every one of them hands it down just as his own inclination prompts. Thus there are as many schemes of "redemption" as there are teachers of these mystical opinions.**[25]

As I read his commentary on the confusing nature of the Gnostic system, I thought about how this is still a phenomenon today. A common and noticeable characteristic of these alternative and "enlightened" ways of seeing Christianity is that people seem to make up anything they want. The more weird and confusing, the better, it seems. Trying to track down some consistency in these cases is nearly impossible. When things seem deep or lofty, they have the veneer of being more impressive, when really they're just weird. Strange. Wrong. Perhaps this is a proven tactic of the devil that still works today.

Whenever a group claims to have a better way of understanding Christianity, it always borrows elements of Christianity and adds extra layers, typically that demand more rule-keeping or an expectation of seeing things in a deeper way, claiming it to be better than classic Christianity. Most forms of New Age thought or generic spirituality fit these criteria.

25 Irenaeus, *Against Heresies*, Book 1, chapter 21, paragraph 1 (*ANF* 1:345). Emphasis in original.

Irenaeus pulls no punches in identifying who is behind Gnostic thought:

> **And when we come to refute them, we shall show in its fitting-place, that this class of men have been instigated by Satan . . .**

He places the blame and origin of this false teaching squarely on the enemy of the triune God and of God's church—on Satan. And Irenaeus drops the Holy Sacrament of Baptism right in the center of what's being denied when one claims God is not using the physical world tied to His Word to provide salvation and the forgiveness of sins. Immediately following the above words, Irenaeus says:

> **. . . to a denial of that baptism which is regeneration to God, and thus to a renunciation of the whole [Christian] faith.**[26]

Wow! Such powerful words! What a brilliant argument. If one says that God cannot assume human flesh, then one is also saying God cannot regenerate or give new life through means, such as the means of Baptism, which is regular water from the earth united with God's Word of promise to save. Notice that Irenaeus is overwhelmingly asserting that Baptism regenerates. He says that Baptism regenerates to God. In other words, through Baptism, one is made alive to God in Christ Jesus (Romans 6:11). One moves from death to life, from darkness to light—all this in Baptism.

This exchange is assumed and proclaimed by Irenaeus as correct Christian teaching over against false teaching parading as Christian teaching. Irenaeus goes further. For Irenaeus—a man who learned

26 Irenaeus, *Against Heresies* 1.21.1 (*ANF* 1:345).

under a student of the apostle John—to deny baptismal regeneration is to deny sound doctrine. Or to say it more potently in Irenaeus's words, to deny baptismal regeneration is "a renunciation of the whole [Christian] faith." He cannot fathom the thought that Baptism does not do what Jesus says it does—make you alive to God. This indeed echoes Jesus' own words in Matthew 28:18–19:

> **And Jesus came and said to them, "All authority in heaven and on earth has been given to Me. Go therefore and make disciples of all nations, baptizing them in the name of the Father and of the Son and of the Holy Spirit."**

Jesus makes one a disciple by Baptism. In Irenaeus's mind, salvation and Baptism are so intrinsically tied together that to deny Jesus coming in the flesh and to deny that Baptism regenerates to God results in the same thing: a denunciation of the entire Christian faith. Irenaeus sees this unbelief and denial of Jesus' own words as satanic. He further states,

> **For the baptism instituted by the visible Jesus was for the remission of sins, but the redemption brought in by that Christ who descended upon Him, was for perfection.**[27]

Irenaeus states that Baptism in plain sight removes the guilt and condemnation inherited by our first parent, Adam. The visible Jesus establishes the visible Word, the Sacraments. This is the clear teaching of Scripture and of the historic Christian faith. To deny this is indeed to align oneself with the Gnostics. For the Gnostics have made salvation come by means of knowledge. May this be a holy warning to us who make Christianity about mere assent to

27 Irenaeus, *Against Heresies* 1.21.2 (*ANF* 1:345).

head knowledge, as if salvation is a higher knowledge that one has achieved over others who are not enlightened.

If Christianity functions like this and gets reduced to a contemplative spirituality, then it moves closer to Gnosticism, the ancestor of that bad idea. As Irenaeus summarizes Gnosticism, he says:

> **For they affirm that the inner and spiritual man is redeemed by means of knowledge, and that they, having acquired the knowledge of all things, stand thenceforth in need of nothing else.**[28]

In denying that God uses the physical world, indeed the water of Baptism, to deliver His gifts of forgiveness, assurance, and comfort, one places oneself at odds with biblical revelation. It converts Christianity into a faith built around the mind and deeper levels of insight, spiritual experiences, and "personal revelation," as many experience in contemporary Charismatic circles.

Speaking of contemporary, Irenaeus thought it important to establish that God using water tied to His Word of healing is not a new idea but an old reality. One can find in the pages of the Old Testament a preview of what was to come concerning Baptism. Irenaeus references Naaman and his cleansing in this fragment dated AD 190:

> **"And [Naaman] dipped himself," says [the Scripture], "seven times in Jordan." It was not for nothing that Naaman of old, when suffering from leprosy, was purified upon his being baptized, but [it served] as an indication to us. For as we are lepers in sin, we are made clean, by means of the sacred water and the**

28 Irenaeus, *Against Heresies* 1.21.4 (*ANF* 1:346).

> **invocation of the Lord, from our old transgressions; being spiritually regenerated as new-born babes, even as the Lord has declared: "Except a man be born again through water and the Spirit, he shall not enter into the kingdom of heaven."[29]**

The statements above are all clear confessions of how the early saints would have understood God's work in Baptism.

May God, by His Holy Spirit given to us in our Baptism, help His church resist the ancient foe, the devil, the liar who spews deadly venom, saying that God would not stoop so low as to use physical means to save sinners. Why resist this notion? As we are learning, God certainly does. It is in His endless wisdom that He has decided to do so. To deny this is ultimately an attack on Jesus Himself and His Body, the church. May we not be numbered among those who deny God's Word. Selah.

Justin Martyr on Baptism

It is much more of a challenge to take God at His Word when you have been reared to run God's Word through a filter first. A filter takes the original thing and offers it back in another form, an alternative way of seeing or experiencing something. Think social media pictures and videos. Typically, filters are understood as an enhancement of the original object. Whether we know it or not, we also do this when we read the Bible or do theology. We filter it. We each bring a bias or a filter to the text and strain the Word of God through it before we walk away with an understanding, typically talked about as "what this passage means to me."

I, too, am guilty of this. I recall being severely turned off on first

29 *Fragments from the Lost Writings of Irenaeus*, Fragment 34 (*ANF* 1:574).

hearing the historic view of Baptism. Offended. Indeed, angered. *How can one teach that Baptism saves? Blasphemy*, I thought! Even after the historic view was explained to me, I still stumbled. One of the barriers for me was that if a person believes by faith that Jesus is who He says He is and that He paid for their sins during His earthly ministry, then at that moment they are saved. Period. No need for any other action.

It sounded like what I was hearing and being told was that Baptism needed to take place before the salvation would be implemented, as if before Baptism the person was in a pseudosalvation or presalvation state. I may not have articulated it using those exact words, but they rightly describe my hesitation and resistance to the concept of baptismal regeneration.

During my time as a student at Concordia Seminary, St. Louis, I kept a skeptical eye and one plugged ear to talks of Baptism as a means of grace. I would always push the conversation to the background and spend little time working through the position being posed. After graduation, I had time to sit with the material on the matter and still found myself struggling to grasp how Baptism as a means of grace did not conflict with and outright contradict justification by faith alone.

I recall a time in one of my counseling classes when Baptism as a means of grace was particularly offensive to me. The professor paired us up and gave us instructions to work through a case study and come to a conclusion on how to resolve a thing based on the material learned up to that point. The person I was grouped with shared a story with me.

He recalled a time when a pastor was confronted about a questionable action. The pastor in the scenario denied the allegations but was eventually proven to be guilty. In this situation, another person shared in the blame. My fellow student went on to say that both he and his spouse were involved in counseling the two people separately once things went public. Unfortunately, during the course of counseling, both parties died an untimely death.

I was floored as my fellow student conveyed this tragedy. What a sad story. More than a story, what a sad loss of life. At the time, I was a staunch five-point Reformed Baptist Calvinist. So many thoughts flooded my mind as I sought to understand what God was up to by taking the lives of the two people involved. On I went with deep theological speculation—something customary and regularly modeled in my circle of theological influence. Finally, I felt I was struck with lofty insight to resolve the mystery of God's sovereign will in this situation.

I proceeded to share with my group member what may have been the root cause of God's decision. I told him God allowed both of the people involved to depart this life to preserve them from further sinning that would cause a loss of rewards or prove that they were never really saved in the first place—particularly, because they both died in their sinful rebellious actions, which led me to conclude that God's action in taking them both may have demonstrated that they were unrepentant and thus unregenerate.

After my lofty, speculative monologue, I noticed the guy looked puzzled, as if I had offered him a riddle to solve that made little sense. I was confused by his confusion. I thought what I said was cogent, brilliant, and simple enough to understand. His long pause eventually started to cast doubt on my personal assessment.

He spoke finally and said something like, "Ummm, I'm not sure about all that, but they both confessed their sin and were in counseling separately to work through the offenses they caused, but beyond that and ultimately, they were baptized. I don't see a need to call their faith into question."

There it was again: Baptism. Baptism being oddly placed in the story. *Why are you bringing up Baptism now, in this awkward part of the episode?* I thought to myself. *What does Baptism have to do with this situation?* Secretly, I thought we were definitely doomed to get a D on this assignment. *This guy thinks Baptism has something to do with salvation*, I complained in my mind. I was sure he was confused and probably misunderstood the assignment.

In real time, unbeknownst to myself, I had placed my interpretive filter over what the Bible says about Baptism. I strained God's Word through my contemporary take on Baptism and assumed it was irrelevant to the subject at hand. Long before then, I had settled for Baptism being simply an outward sign of an inward change, an outward expression of what God does in the heart. So for my group member to make it the conclusion, indeed the hope of salvation, was the most clumsy thing ever to me.

For him, Baptism was a reality that God the Son implanted into His plan to save sinners and to mark them as His own, a thing I hadn't come to grips with yet. He focused more on the offenses and the way forward concerning neighbor, or the people involved. I placed the focus on God's eternal decrees dating back to "eternity past" and God's plan of election and damnation. In short, he was right. I was wrong. He understood the assignment. I did not.

Looking back, I see how comforting the doctrine of Baptism is. Rightly understood, it is uniquely helpful in the counseling room. It addresses the person as sinner and saint. It confronts the person's wrongdoings and their forgiveness. It applies to their identity and their responsibility moving forward in a fallen world. It anchors the person and sets them free at the same time. Yet I was still perplexed by this question: If Baptism delivers forgiveness of sins, then are people in a holding pattern until they hit the water and hear the invocation of the triune name?

Although my group member implied that hope and assurance of salvation are also benefits of the Sacrament, rooted in God's work in Baptism, I hadn't connected the dots yet. I was still collecting them, trying to make sense of what felt like a bizarre concept that I thought Lutherans had invented. I left class that day deeply impacted by our exchange, and I have not forgotten it to this day. I recall it often when thinking about the origins of my exploration of what Baptism truly is. The sheer power of our theological paradigm clash caused me to wonder more about Baptism and how he and I could have such radically different views of the rite.

One of the primary barriers to my embrace of the historic view of Baptism was the notion that salvation is this one-dimensional thing that happens in your head in a defining moment. Coming up in the generic American church, I typically heard about a person's "testimony" or their "conversion experience," as it's called in some circles. Mostly, it's structured like this: I grew up in the church. I strayed away or backslid. Got involved in some bad things that I knew I shouldn't have, and after a dramatic experience, I felt God trying to get my attention and calling me back home. Then I responded, or answered the call. After that, I got baptized as my first act of obedience.

With that construct fixed in my mind, I had no space for baptismal regeneration. No placement for it in a way that would couple Baptism with salvation. It belonged tacked on the back end as an act of obedience that I perform to show Jesus that I passed my first test or responded to His Law properly by getting dunked in the water and showing the world I was not afraid to be associated with Jesus and Christianity. It signaled to God and others that I was serious for the first time. Or in many cases, serious yet again after straying away for a time.

The above paradigm is so widely practiced among mainline Protestants that it would be a miracle if you learned of another way. There is little to no chance that the average Christian raised in an American Evangelical church would ever hear about baptismal regeneration—the ancient and original way. The only exception to the rule might be by some exposure to Roman Catholicism. Even if that's the case, Catholics have been so royally branded by Evangelical circles as lost or not even Christians that the idea would be readily dismissed as demonic.

However, if or when a person would miraculously get exposed to ancient expressions of Christian conversion and Baptism, they'd notice the process was a bit different from our contemporary one. The ancient way challenges the way modern Evangelicals understand how a person gets saved. The go-to biblical pattern for modern Evangelicals is mostly based on Romans 10:9:

> **If you confess with your mouth that Jesus is Lord and believe in your heart that God raised Him from the dead, you will be saved.**

Paul's words are used as a rigid formula for getting people saved, as if Paul had nothing to say about Baptism being tied to salvation. This happens when people do not understand how to work through the Bible. As if the Bible contradicts itself or is not a coherent book that supports itself and centers around Jesus, the baptizer (see

John 4:1–2). Romans 10:9 provides zero defense against baptismal regeneration. It does not cancel the work God does in Baptism. It does not eliminate the need to be baptized for the forgiveness of sins (Acts 2:38) or to enter into the kingdom of God (John 3:5).

When I encountered St. Justin the Martyr and his heroic defense of the Christian faith, I was floored. His arguments were culturally relevant to his day and provided a clear and helpful defense of the Christian religion, an intelligent one that proved the validity of the faith being called into question. Can you guess what Justin saw fit to include in his defense of biblical Christianity to an audience of non-Christians and Jews? Yes, Baptism.

Okay, I'm getting ahead of myself. Let's discover a bit more about our dear brother. Justin Martyr was born around AD 100 in Flavia Neapolis, which is in modern-day Nablus, West Bank. He was one of the earliest and most important Christian apologists, that is, a defender of the faith. His life and works played a major role in defending and explaining the Christian religion to a largely pagan audience during the second century. He helps us understand the early church's interaction with the surrounding Greco-Roman world and its ideas.

Justin was born into a pagan family, as he himself states, and was well educated in the philosophies of his day. He studied various schools of thought, including Platonism, Pythagoreanism, Stoicism, and Aristotelianism. After spending time engaging all those philosophical systems, he found them ultimately unsatisfying in answering the weightier questions of existence and life. His search for ultimate truth led him to Christianity, which he embraced after being deeply impacted by the steadfastness of Christians facing persecution and by the teachings of Jesus, the Christ.

Following his conversion to Christianity, the Martyr continued to wear the philosopher's cloak, a symbol of his dedication to the pursuit of truth. Nevertheless, his philosophy was now rooted in Christian teaching. He traveled widely, teaching and contending for Christianity in major cities, such as Rome and Ephesus. His interactions and apologies targeted both pagan philosophers and Roman authorities, whom he sought to win to the rationality and truth of the Christian faith.

Justin is mostly famous for his writings *The First Apology*, *The Second Apology*, and *Dialogue with Trypho*. In them, he systematically defended Christianity against charges of atheism, refuted accusations of immorality, and demonstrated the harmony between reason and faith. He addressed *The First Apology* to Emperor Antoninus Pius. In it, he provides a description of Christian worship and beliefs, one of the earliest detailed descriptions we have, even including descriptions of the Eucharist and Baptism.

Dialogue with Trypho offers a recounting of a fictional conversation with a Jewish philosopher, in which he argues that Jesus is the Anointed One and the fulfillment of Old Covenant prophecies. This work is an early example of Christian-Jewish dialogue and demonstrates Justin's great understanding of both Jewish and Christian writings.

Justin's life came to a dramatic yet triumphant end around AD 165. During a period of immense persecution under Emperor Marcus Aurelius, Justin was arrested, along with some of his students, for refusing to sacrifice to the Roman gods. He was threatened with torture and death, but boldly declared, "Through prayer we can be saved on account of our Lord Jesus Christ, even when we have been punished, because this shall become to us salvation and confidence at the more fearful and universal judgment-seat of our Lord and Saviour."[30] Justin and his disciples were beheaded, resulting in his title "Martyr" and placing him among the great saints of the church.

In Justin's *First Apology*, he defends Christian Baptism against Greek thought and heathen religiosity and rightly ties it to salvation. They belong hand in hand in his mind, according to Scripture and his own study of the church's teachings and proclamation. I find it fascinating that Baptism is considered a strong apologetic to ancient defenders of the faith. For Justin, God's work in Baptism strengthens the Christian claim. It demonstrates God's love and salvific plan for humanity, that God would wash away sins and bring sinners into His kingdom.

Justin says this about Baptism:

> **As many as are persuaded and believe that what we teach and say is true, and undertake to be able to live accordingly, are instructed to pray and to entreat God with fasting, for the remission of their sins that are past, we praying and fasting with them. Then they are brought by us where there is water, and are regenerated in the same manner in which we were ourselves regenerated. For, in the name of God, the Father and Lord of the universe, and our Savior Jesus Christ, and of the Holy Spirit, they then receive the washing with water. For Christ also said, "Except ye be born again, ye shall not enter into the kingdom of heaven."[31]**

30 Justin Martyr, *The Martyrdom of the Holy Martyrs*, chapter 4 (*ANF* 1:306).
31 *The First Apology of Justin*, chapter 61 (*ANF* 1:183).

Wow! Beautiful words from our second-century brother, only one century removed from Jesus and the apostles. Yet another church father teaching that Baptism regenerates when done in the precious name of the Father, the Son, and the Holy Spirit, teaching that God makes one alive and unites them in Christ upon Baptism. Justin even references John 3:3–5, which says,

> **Jesus answered him, "Truly, truly, I say to you, unless one is born again he cannot see the kingdom of God." Nicodemus said to Him, "How can a man be born when he is old? Can he enter a second time into his mother's womb and be born?" Jesus answered, "Truly, truly, I say to you, unless one is born of water and the Spirit, he cannot enter the kingdom of God."**

Indeed, the waters of Baptism and the Spirit unite to graft one into Christ's Body, the church.

Another thing to observe in Justin's description of Baptism above is the preparation that persons underwent before receiving Baptism. People interested in becoming a Christian or "being saved," as we say, did a few things leading up to Baptism:

- They were persuaded and believed.
- They undertook to live accordingly.
- They prayed and entreated God with fasting for forgiveness.
- They were accompanied in fasting and prayer by the leaders.

- They were finally brought to the water and regenerated.

The contemporary insistence that the only way into the faith is that one merely has a dramatic experience or an epiphany and then believes in their heart, confesses Jesus is Lord with their mouth, either gets baptized or not, then *bam!* they are saved is not the ancient way. Nor was Baptism slapped on after belief as a declaration of the person's new commitment to and relationship with their personal Lord and Savior. No. Justin spoke of Baptism as a means of God delivering grace. He saw learning, prayer, and fasting as a part of Christian life toward that end.

To be clear, Baptism is not expressed as an empty symbol but as a miracle taking place using water and God's work of regeneration. Justin also states,

> **Even as our Christ, by being crucified on the tree, and by purifying [us] with water, has redeemed us, though plunged in the direst offences which we have committed, and has made [us] a house of prayer and adoration.**[32]

Again, the events of Jesus' earthly ministry are joined with Baptism: "by purifying [us] with water, has redeemed us." One simply clings to the promise God gives in Baptism and receives the benefits of forgiveness and purification. Further in the *Dialogue*, Justin states,

> **For righteous Noah, along with the other mortals at the deluge, i.e., with his own wife, his three sons**

32 Justin Martyr, *Dialogue with Trypho*, chapter 86 (*ANF* 1:242).

> and their wives, being eight in number, were a symbol of the eighth day, wherein Christ appeared when He rose from the dead, for ever the first in power. For Christ, being the first-born of every creature, became again the chief of another race regenerated by Himself through water, and faith, and wood, containing the mystery of the cross; even as Noah was saved by wood when he rode over the waters with his household. . . . I mean, that by water, faith, and wood, those who are afore-prepared, and who repent of the sins which they have committed, shall escape from the impending judgment of God.[33]

Just wow! This is beautifully stated.

Ignatius of Antioch on Baptism

I love Ignatius's emphasis on the unity of the church and his biblical instruction to honor the bishop. For him, this impacted sound doctrine, unity in the church, and the proper understanding and usage of the Sacraments, not for vain purposes or for personal gain. Submitting to authority is a struggle for us these days. In our context, people get skittish when asked to submit to authority—in some cases, due to abuses from authority figures, rightfully so. Or they submit without any clarity of understanding or scrutiny of what they are submitting to. Both are incorrect.

I recall a time as a teenager attending a particular church when the bishop, as he was called, had a guest speaker preach during

33 Justin Martyr, *Dialogue with Trypho*, chapter 138 (*ANF* 1:268).

a conference. The room was jam-packed. Wall to wall. The guest preacher was extremely popular, a well-respected prophet among the denomination. We all anticipated what he would speak on and waited to hear what specific word from God he had for us as a church body and maybe even what word God would offer to a few special individuals. I remember the service started at 7:00 p.m. As I pulled up to the church parking lot, it was loaded. Nearly full.

Happily, there were a few spots left. I parallel parked as fast as I could to hopefully grab a seat. As I walked into the building, I recall being taken aback by all the people dressed to impress and singing with such joy and exuberance. I scanned the room for any familiar faces so I could find a seat and at least sit next to a friend. Yes! I spotted one of my bros and, embarrassed, scooted my way through the pew to the middle section where he was seated. Finally, I was in. I had blended into the room, and the anxiety of being seen was all behind me.

I joined in the singing but mostly anticipated the sermon. As an introvert, I was never much into the boisterous style of praise and worship. I felt like I always suffered through it and tried to make the most of it. Still, I was happy for everyone else who could get lost in the "charismania" of it all. Itching for the sermon, I prayed and asked God for "a word" that He would speak to me through the message and affirm whether or not He heard me when I prayed. To affirm that He saw my efforts to live holy and to be a good witness for Jesus in my community and in all my dealings.

Looking over the heads of the people sitting in front of me, I hoped to lay eyes on the guest speaker. There he was, walking in from the pastor's office and into the pulpit, robed in his purple and gold vestments, glasses on his face, and a Bible in his hand. He stood about five-foot-six but carried himself like a giant. As the singing tapered off, our pastor approached the podium to introduce him to the congregation. The chitter-chatter was loud, as most people already knew who the guest was and his style of preaching and prophesying.

When the guest speaker finally took the podium, he greeted us with a warm welcome from both himself and his church congregation in the name of our Lord Jesus, the Christ. As he paced back and forth encouraging us, expositing passages from the Old Testament, and proclaiming blessings over us, he made it clear he had a special word from God for us. "So listen up," he said. The moment we were waiting on! A prophecy, special revelation, and insight directly from God to the mouth of the bishop. Well, at least that's how we understood it then.

He told us God said to say that for the remaining days of that year, we ought to follow our pastor wherever he went to preach. Whenever our pastor opened his mouth to preach, we needed to be there. Even if it was out of town, it did not matter. Each and every member was required to be there. According to him, this is what God told him to tell us during the conference.

He told us—based, he claimed, on revelation from God—that in every sermon our pastor would give for the rest of that year, we would receive clear instruction for the things each one of us inquired about from God. That God would make things plain and apparent for each individual. We would receive instructions, insights, and warnings from God through the mouth of His servant. If you happened to miss an occasion, then you would also miss answers and instructions from God.

This message was received with loud shouts of praise and thanksgiving. On its face, it sounded like a helpful thing. For each inquiry you have before God in prayer, simply go hear our pastor guest speak and hear him regularly at service. Then you'll get specific answers delivered from God. Easy, right? I can even remember taking a road trip to a church where our pastor had to speak. Both my friend and I went in anticipation of our particular "word." While sitting and listening to him preach, I struggled to connect the dots between the message and my personal experience. So did my friend.

We both laughed about it in the car. "Man, I have no clue what God was saying to me tonight!" we joked. We chalked it up to some deficiency in us because we knew God makes zero mistakes. Nevertheless, we were not discouraged or ready to give up. We followed him to a second church venue a week later, hoping to hear a fresh "word" from God.

Yet again, same thing as last time, vague principles to apply but nothing concrete or specific to my life's needs at the time. Nothing like the "prophet" promised that day, a guaranteed specific "word" for each individual. Only more ambiguity and universal principles preached. I could not make the third trip for one reason or another. Eventually, I stopped trying because if I missed the first two specific "words" preached, I figured I was royally off track by then. I concluded that God had given up on me since I couldn't connect the dots from the first two sermons, not to mention missing the third occasion. *Oh well. I guess I'll figure things out some other way*, I determined.

I continued to show up for Sunday morning worship. There, I would attend and listen intently for this "word" God promised us. As if it were yesterday, I remember how the nature of the sermons shifted from a focus on reaching the community for Jesus, living rightly, and honoring God with holy living to more of a prosperity emphasis. Prosperity mixed with more of a focal point on emotional and mystical experience. A book on how to "chase God" was introduced to us. It promised a closer walk with God with more evidence of supernatural power. More victory over life's obstacles and favor from God to access more material things here on earth.

From there, the sermons began to call on the church to offer more money to God. To sacrifice more for the sake of the Kingdom, it was said. One Sunday, the pastor formed multiple lines for churchgoers to line up. There was a twenty-dollar line, a fifty-dollar line, and a hundred-dollar line. We were all encouraged to find a line that best fit our financial situation. The pastor asked who desired to be a millionaire. Hands were raised all over the building. He then taught that the way to riches was to give.

I can hear the sermon now as the pastor quoted Luke 6:38 to say that if you give what you have to the church, then riches would follow—provided your lifestyle was up to par. He would hold the mic close to his mouth and quote the King James Version of the passage, using it to offer a promise of financial prosperity:

> **Give, and it shall be given unto you; good measure, pressed down, and shaken together, and running over, shall men give into your bosom.** (KJV)

The pianist picked up on the enthusiasm of the pastor and began to play. Next, the guitarist picked up on it and strummed a bass line. Then the drummer joined in and kicked off a cadence. All in a matter of a moment, the room erupted with shouts and dance. People poured out of the aisles and into one of the lines to make an offering unto the Lord.

The stakes were raised. The pastor told the congregation that if they gave up full paychecks to the church that month, that God would bless some tenfold, some twentyfold, and some a hundredfold, a blessing of healing, a financial blessing, or with the desires of one's heart. More praise ensued, accompanied by sweet melodies from the musicians. The lines began to fill, and so did the purse of that day. It was indeed a spectacle.

As I sat back and observed the room, it felt eerie. I had never witnessed this type of debacle during a service before, at least not there. The lion's share of my time there had been different. The pastor normally preached the Bible as simply and plainly as he could. His normal approach was most helpful and was used greatly in my Christian formation as a young man. Never had I heard my pastor so hyped up on Charismatic homiletics. He was like an entirely different person at that time.

I thought about the "prophecy" from the guest speaker during the conference. He told us to follow every "word" from our pastor and said that every "word" he would preach would be the exact "word" from God Himself for our congregation. In that moment, I decided that something was off in a major way. I didn't have the depth of theological language to describe it, but it felt eerie and wrong. I decided within myself that day that I could no longer take the pastor's words to be that of God. I could not bring myself to comply with this brand of submission to the bishop or the office itself, if that was what it was.

In stark contrast, Ignatius of Antioch meant an entirely different thing while championing the office of bishop. *Who is this Ignatius in the first place?* I can hear you asking. Good question. He was born in the middle of the first century, the same century as our Lord Jesus and the disciples. In fact, Ignatius knew the apostles and even engaged with them personally. It is recorded that the apostle John was his teacher. He was born in Syria, where he eventually became the third bishop of Antioch, the same place the apostle Peter served as bishop, according to tradition. Ignatius was a bold witness for the faith.

As a pastor, he contributed much to those he served and left a legacy worth knowing about and commemorating. Most memorable would be the seven epistles he wrote, most to different communities of Christians and one to Polycarp, another major figure who had been discipled by John. Ignatius wrote these letters en route to Rome, where he was sentenced to death by the Roman Emperor Trajan and martyred as food for wild beasts in the Roman Colosseum.

Filled with faith as his life hung in the balance, Ignatius makes this statement to the brothers and sisters in the church of Rome:

> **I write to the Churches, and impress on them all, that I shall willingly die for God, unless ye hinder me. I beseech of you not to show an unseasonable good-will towards me. Suffer me to become food for the wild beasts, through whose instrumentality it will be granted me to attain to God.**[34]

Sheesh, I cannot imagine being in that position, but I pray that if I'm ever called to lay down my life for the sake of the Good News of Jesus that I would be filled with such faith. Ignatius took discipleship seriously and wanted to be like our Lord Jesus even to the point of death. He valued the cost Jesus paid for His Bride and wanted to live and die in a manner worthy of it. This speaks to why he upheld the office of bishop so highly. It was an office Jesus established to deliver His Word and the visible Word, the Sacraments.

34 *Epistle of Ignatius to the Romans*, chapter 4 (*ANF* 1:75).

For Ignatius, the bishop was put in place by Jesus to preserve the unity of the church and her precious teachings:

> **See that ye all follow the bishop, even as Jesus Christ does the Father, and the presbytery as ye would the apostles; and reverence the deacons, as being the institution of God.[35]**

Brilliant! If God instituted it, it is good. If God calls the offices good, then they must be regarded as such. But this could become a challenge for us if we reduce the Sacraments to a mere picture of a past work Jesus did for us. If that's all they are, they don't demand the same reverence for them or for those presiding over them. They are no longer mysterious happenings administered by the bishop or pastor.

If preaching is reduced to motivational speeches or therapeutic pep talks, parishioners soon realize they don't need to go to church to experience either one of those things. They can listen to positive affirmations on an app. They can push up on a podcast that pumps them up. Who needs a bishop for that? After all, that one guy who started a podcast makes good points, too, and has a big personality that keeps people's attention. Plus, he goes viral often and that makes it less embarrassing to share with friends.

Bishops, though? They are too preachy when they stick to the Word of God and Sacraments. Even with a great camera, great lighting and audio, current editing styles, and music blended in perfectly, the bishop expanding on the Bible rightly still trails behind the podcaster giving commentary on trending topics. Pop-culture Christianity has fashioned the Christian appetite for sweets only as opposed to a well-balanced meal with sweets on the side.

35 *Epistle of Ignatius to the Smyrnaeans*, chapter 8 (*ANF* 1:89).

Ignatius goes on to say in the same letter,

> **It is well to reverence both God and the bishop. He who honours the bishop has been honoured by God; he who does anything without the knowledge of the bishop, does [in reality] serve the devil.**[36]

This is indeed a startling statement, particularly to a people who pride themselves on individualism. I'm thinking of a mainstream podcaster who invited a Christian on to talk about matters of religion and the church. The podcaster shared his disagreement and disdain that the church insisted on a mediator. This host simply did not like the idea of going through someone "to get to God." For many, Jesus Himself stands in the way, and most certainly a bishop does too. Others even claim to be okay with Jesus but would prefer not to have any dealings with His church. For those types, they mostly lead with their personal experience—usually a bad one—and never let the church return to a place of innocence in their minds.

You hear things like "I'm cool with Jesus, but the church is filled with hypocrites. That's why I have my own relationship with God. I don't need to go to church to have a personal relationship with Him." While this type of talk is more than commonplace and I understand how someone can end up with this mindset, it is not helpful. Nor is it evidence of actually being in a relationship with Jesus. I liken that type of talk to a guy who has a great friendship with someone but doesn't like his friend's wife. He says things like "I'm cool with you, but your wife is a hypocrite. She's mean, has a nasty attitude, and is hard to get along with, but you're my bro! I love you."

That may be understandable on some level. Perhaps the guy had

36 *Epistle of Ignatius to the Smyrnaeans*, chapter 9 (*ANF* 1:90). Brackets in original.

a bad experience with the wife. Maybe she was his boss and fired him, for example. But if he constantly shares his disapproval and disdain for his friend's wife, at some point, the friend with the wife is going to question their relationship. The friend will eventually push for reconciliation if they are to remain friends. However, if the guy refuses to reconcile with the wife and continues to belabor how terrible she is, then that will inevitably damage the friendship, if not sever it altogether.

All that to say, if you refuse to honor the offices and means of grace Jesus established for the good of His church and you still wish to lay hold of the benefits of salvation earned by Jesus, then at some point, you should bend your will. Bend it toward Jesus' Word and resist your personal preferences against what Jesus determined is good for you. The church is Jesus' Bride, and no man—indeed, not even the God-man—will tolerate forever you trashing His Bride.

Ignatius is clear on this. Throughout his letters, he constantly makes this point and insists on the good nature of God's intentions behind the bishopric. When writing to the Smyrnaeans, he brings Baptism into the discussion:

> **Wherever the bishop shall appear, there let the multitude [of the people] also be; even as, wherever Jesus Christ is, there is the Catholic Church. It is not lawful without the bishop either to baptize or to celebrate a love-feast; but whatsoever he shall approve of, that is also pleasing to God, so that everything that is done may be secure and valid.**[37]

37 *Epistle of Ignatius to the Smyrnaeans*, chapter 8 (*ANF* 1:90). Brackets in original.

Beautiful! In this one statement, a lot is said. Ignatius establishes that the church should rally around the Word of God, which Jesus put the bishop in place to proclaim.

Ignatius realizes, like all Christians at this time, that Baptism is a miraculous act of God that brings one into the church, which inherently means into a saving relationship with Jesus. Therefore, he commits the role of baptizing to the bishop, the one ordained by Jesus and given the vocation to proclaim the Word to the church, including the visible Word, the Sacraments. Yet, because of the priesthood of all the saints, Ignatius gives a caveat when he says, "But whatsoever he shall approve of, that is also pleasing to God, so that everything that is done may be secure and valid." Clearly, he is concerned with proper order and the comfort of consciences among the saints, which sounds like another could baptize or host a love-feast, given the right qualifications. Such a beautiful pastoral concern.

I love how the Antioch pastor refers to Baptism here. He yet again ties the Sacraments to the office of bishop and the church's unity. However, this time he adds a more poignant point to what Baptism is and does:

> **Give ye heed to the bishop, that God also may give heed to you. My soul be for theirs that are submissive to the bishop, to the presbyters, and to the deacons, and may my portion be along with them in God! Labour together with one another; strive in company together; run together; suffer together; sleep together; and awake together, as the stewards, and associates, and servants of God. Please ye Him under whom ye fight, and from whom ye receive**

> **your wages. Let none of you be found a deserter. Let your baptism endure as your arms; your faith as your helmet.**[38]

People who hold the position that Baptism is an outward sign of an inward change mostly have no language or category for speaking of Baptism as something relevant to your day-to-day affairs in the faith. I rarely hear anyone who holds a metaphorical view of the rite referencing their Baptism as a useful reference point for common occurrences as a Christian.

The conversation surrounding Baptism usually comes from expressions of Christianity that understand Baptism to be what Paul says it is. What Jesus says it is. A real death and resurrection in the water. As confessional Lutherans emphasize, Baptism is the identity of the Christian. Believers in Jesus live the baptized life, dying to sin and being raised to new life daily. Indeed, Christians are the baptized, those who are marked by Jesus and washed clean of their sins. In this truth, there is comfort, assurance, and protection.

After discovering how widespread and unanimous the teaching of baptismal regeneration was during the earliest stages of Christian history, it makes perfect sense to understand Ignatius's words that way. He says, "Let your baptism endure as your arms!" This short sentence is bursting with significance and meaning. It does not sound like he understands Baptism as a mere word picture for a past act of Jesus. No, it's a present reality empowered by the miracle performed by God when you went under the water and were brought back up as the triune God's name was invoked in the presence of His Holy Spirit.

---

38 *Epistle of Ignatius to Polycarp*, chapter 6 (*ANF* 1:95).

If Baptism endures as your arms, your weaponry and protective gear, then according to pastor and teacher Ignatius, Baptism saves you. In an ongoing way. Where does the power to do so come from? Is it magic? Are there salvific properties in the water? Not at all. Baptism is empowered by Jesus and His work that He performs in the water. As Ignatius teaches,

> **He was born and was baptized by John, that He might ratify the institution committed to that prophet.**[39]

Ignatius credits Jesus for the work of Baptism, saying that the work being done in each Baptism will be valid because of Jesus' own Baptism, which purifies the water, thus ratifying the institution. Therefore, from here on out, all those entering into the water in His name, by faith only, will endure in protection with arms against sin and death. Yes, in their Baptism as the baptized. Amen.

This is the truth of God the bishops are to proclaim and feed to Jesus' sheep. Nothing else. The words of Ignatius quoted earlier bring it full circle: "That is also pleasing to God." Ignatius said you can only follow a bishop's message and work if it is "pleasing to God." Not if it merely draws a crowd. Not if it comes from an attractive person. Not if it comes from someone bearing the name *bishop* but teaching contrary to the apostles' teachings. Only honor the bishops who are doing and saying what is "pleasing to God": His Word, His church, and His Sacraments.

Earlier in this chapter, I shared my experience with another bishop—not Bishop Ignatius, but one whose activity contradicted Scripture and did not cultivate unity among the saints. Activity that was not consistent with the creeds of the church. A bishop of a

39 *Epistle of Ignatius to the Ephesians*, chapter 18 (*ANF* 1:57).

congregation that was instructed, by a "prophet," to adhere to every word and sermon from said bishop in order to hear from God what He would say to the church.

Unfortunately, and with all due respect, the bishop was not in alignment at that time with the teachings of the church. Let's hope things are better now. Nevertheless, at that time, it was right and good to give an enduring effort to prayer and to mentioning the points of concern. As a young deacon, I was given such a position and license to respectfully and tenderly do so. Met with much resistance and intolerance, I had to make an exit. Without making a scene or causing unnecessary or harmful division, I stepped down from my position and removed my membership from that congregation. The journey continued.

CHAPTER 5

THE EUCHARIST ACCORDING TO THE EARLY CHURCH

I confess, the most impactful doctrine I learned about during my studies for my master's degree concerned the Lord's Supper. While testing into the program, I read on an array of topics that were new to me. Some, though familiar, were newly put. Reading, for the first time, about Baptism and the way it's always been understood from the first century forward was overwhelming. It was discussed and taught in such a different way that it completely scrambled my mind on the matter. So much so that I sort of ignored it for a while. However, I gave much energy and attention to the study of the Lord's Supper.

I was utterly befuddled by the claim that Jesus was bodily present in the earthly elements of bread and wine. No such claim had ever hit my human eardrums. I hadn't been exposed to this understanding of the Eucharist before. In fact, I hadn't even heard the word *Eucharist* used prior to then. If I had, it would have been such a distant memory that it was as if it never happened.

I was so offended by the concept that I deeply questioned my inclination to enroll into the institution. While reading about this claim, I became angry. I put the book down for a second to seriously consider if I should back out of the registration process. How can anyone have the audacity to outright uproot the teaching of Communion and turn it into such a superstitious and spooky one?

Is there really this little respect for the holiness and grandeur of our infinite triune God on this campus?

With that much vehement horror and disdain for the ancient claim, what made me continue to go through with my interest in studying in such a place? In one sense, I don't know. It was beyond me. In another sense, thinking back, I was so desperate for any little hope that Christianity was true. The claim of "real presence" was so grippingly strange that it made me curious. That there was a "mystical union" taking place in the Meal was exactly bold enough to garner my exploration. I pondered deeply about the nature of a people who could share such a passion for Jesus and His Word but who could so easily embrace what I thought was a clear misunderstanding of the Lord's Supper.

I pushed forward and put my grave suspicions to the side in order to see what I might find in this strange land. While sitting in class listening to Dr. Robert A. Kolb lecture on the Lord's Supper, I was all ears. Notepad, ink pen, and iPhone Voice Memos recording. What was in my heart and mind at the time, remember, was desperation or any little hope that Christianity was true. I enrolled into the graduate program as a last-ditch effort to see if there was an abiding love and real rescue for weak and helpless sinners such as myself.

At that stage of my life, I had given eighteen years of training and formation to examining my heart's affections and inner motivations. Monitoring my thoughts and potential thoughts. Scrutinizing my desires and speculating on what God was thinking about my inner life. Wondering about His perfect gaze at all my private thoughts, feelings, and passions. Afraid of when He would strike as a result of His perfect and clear awareness of all that runs through my mind and imagination.

This was commonplace and regularly discussed among the church culture I was in at the time. As a Calvinist from the Reformed Baptist wing, we lived there: ever present before God's eye and earnestly striving to show Him our sincere desire to overcome our vile, corrupt nature. Gnawingly inspecting our motivations. *Why do I truly want this job opportunity? Is it because I want to be rich and am not wholly living for God's glory but my own? Why do I actually want to marry this person? Is it because she is attractive and well known in our Bible study, or do I genuinely want to love her like Christ loved the church? Did I prepare and preach that sermon to show how well read I am or because I wholeheartedly love God's people and want them to get closer to God?*

This is what I and countless others in that camp experience(d) as our daily inner voice. Some of them are close friends and are still entangled in such a web. Others have jumped ship altogether and left Christianity because of the throat-choking nature of such a terribly tight theological grip. Desperate for relief, one goes after major spiritual exploits to appease God. You seek after "ministry opportunities" to offset this mischaracterization of God's negative disposition toward you. Things like sharing your faith with strangers at the barbershop or beauty salon. Taking a mission trip to help those who live in poverty. Opening your home to the homeless. Starting a Bible study on campus. All good things but performed for not-so-good reasons, done to signal to God that you know how dirty you are but are hoping through such efforts that He will see that you desire to be a good, clean Christian.

Now, back to class with Dr. Kolb. I'm sitting there with the above-mentioned exhaustion, filtering his lecture through my many layers of spiritual fatigue. As he's sharing his joy-filled points about real presence, I'm struggling to grasp why he's so happy about it. He's making mention of the sheer blessing of participating in the Divine Service, where Jesus serves us with His body and blood through bread and wine.

To me, at the time, it sounded like more Law. More rules. *So now I have to go to church because I need to receive Communion more regularly? God will be mad at me for missing a Sunday because I wasn't able to take Communion? Great. Do more stuff or else God will get mad again.* You can probably feel the negative weight of my thinking at the time as you are reading this. Good. That feeling is there because it was the filter I had distorting the sweetness of the eucharistic reality that Dr. Kolb proclaimed. Many others experience the same thing when they hear of the beautiful blessing of the Supper, but it gets overcast by the dark cloud of their confusion.

I needed more clarity. I raised my hand to ask the prof a question. He glanced over and said, "Yes, Marcus, you have a question or comment?"

"Yeah, I do," I replied.

I began by looking at Matthew 26:26–29:

> **Now as they were eating, Jesus took bread, and after blessing it broke it and gave it to the disciples, and said, "Take, eat; this is My body." And He took a cup, and when He had given thanks He gave it to them, saying, "Drink of it, all of you, for this is My blood of the covenant, which is poured out for many for the forgiveness of sins. I tell you I will not drink again of this fruit of the vine until that day when I drink it new with you in My Father's kingdom."**

"You're saying that Jesus is saying the bread *is* His body and the wine *is* His blood? That He is not saying that those elements represent what He is about to undergo on the cross for our sins?"

To which the dear professor replied, "I didn't say it; Jesus did. But yes."

"But how?" I followed up.

"That's just what Jesus said. We take Him at His Word."

I must come clean; that was the most intellectually unsatisfying answer I had ever heard in my life. Even though Dr. Kolb was 100 percent correct, I wanted more. Jesus' words weren't satisfying enough, sad to say. I had grown accustomed to persons with "Dr." tacked on to the front of their names answering Bible questions with lengthy spiels and lofty speculations, at least dropping a few options to consider concerning what God may have had in mind. Or suggesting several plausible philosophical explanations for such inscrutable truths.

I wasn't done. "Dr. Kolb, I have another question," I interjected. He gestured for me to continue. "If Jesus is saying the bread is His body and the wine is His blood, as you say, then wouldn't Jesus be saying that the cup itself is His blood, not the wine?" I proceeded to read the text aloud. "The passage actually says, 'And He took a cup, and when He had given thanks He gave it to them, saying, "Drink of it, all of you, for this is My blood."' It appears that the 'this' is the cup He was holding. That's what He referred to as His blood, the cup. Not the wine in the cup, apparently."

The room went silent. The question sounded like I was being a jerk or seeking for a "gotchu" moment. I promise you, I genuinely wasn't. I was attempting to apply the literal hermeneutic or interpretation style to the text that I thought Dr. Kolb was applying.

Another student interrupted the cold silence and said aloud,

"Yeah, what do we say to that?"

I was so happy when he shouted that out, because I didn't want it to come across as if I was seeking to stump the professor.

With such gentleness, the dear doctor said that the cup would have been understood grammatically as a way of referring to the wine. As the text goes on to make plain: "I tell you I will not drink again of this fruit of the vine. . . ."

The assigned readings from Pieper's *Christian Dogmatics* would go on to confirm this:

> **That the Lutherans understand by the "cup" not the vessel, but the wine contained in the cup; hence metonymically [. . .]. Hodge says: "When Christ says, 'This cup is the New Testament,' it is admitted that the cup is used metonymically for the wine in the cup." Yes, but thus we are abiding by the words of institution, for Christ tells us to drink not the cup, but of the cup: "Drink ye all of it [. . .]," Matt. 26:27. And Scripture expressly reports that the disciples complied with the instruction of Christ and drank, not the cup, but of the cup: "And they all drank of it" (Mark 14:23).**[40]

In that moment, I knew all confessional Lutherans were crazy. Crazy enough to take Jesus at His Word. Crazy enough to hold fast to the precious revelation of Scripture and not to fold under the pressure of skepticism bombarding and begging them to back down. I was further intrigued. Truthfully, one of the most impactful

40 Francis Pieper, *Christian Dogmatics*, vol. 3 (Concordia Publishing House, 1953), 345.

things about the claim was Jesus' words "for many for the forgiveness of sins." *Could this mean what it says? Does Jesus apply forgiveness in the Meal?*

Let me read it again, I thought. *Maybe I'm missing something. Overlooking something or reading too fast. No, that's what it says: "for the forgiveness of sins." Wow! Why have I never noticed that?* It was as if an angel hurried up and wrote it in while my head was turned. I still wasn't ready to allow myself to see what I had just seen, but I do recall the encounter chiseling away at my hardened heart, just enough to let a little ray of light shine in.

The Inner Life

I was that person on campus: in seminary but scared of God. Ruthlessly looking within to find something pure and holy to offer to Him but not able to track it down. Yet I was discipled to acknowledge how hideous my inner life was, called to purify my inner life, and taught to then depend on my inner life for assurance of salvation. How can all three of these things be done? They are each equally daunting. One author told us that our inner life is like a barrel of TNT sticks (old-school bombs). He said that all humans are like sitting barrels filled with TNT sticks. All it takes is one spark, and BOOM! A huge explosion!

One wrong move. One wrong decision. One fall into sin and BOOM! Your career can be brought to an end. Your family can be destroyed. He expressed that Christians are always under a soul-threatening explosion if they mess up their one chance to do things right. Although this popular Calvinist author affirmed justification by faith alone, he also believed in and taught double predestination (that God chose some for heaven and others for hell) and limited atonement (that Jesus did not die for everyone without exception). Therefore, the threat was that you can live an entire life thinking you are a Christian but then get to heaven's gates and be shocked and surprised by the sad news that you were deceived. By your own self-deception, you thought you were a Christian but never actually were one in the first place.

All those years of Bible reading, prayer, sharing your faith, denying the flesh, listening to sermons and only Christian music. Turning R-rated movies off when inappropriate scenes were shown. Sacrificing time and talent doing good in the world. And BOOM Jesus tells you to depart from Him, for He never knew you. Sends chills down my spine just thinking about that terrible and tragic understanding and unfortunate articulation of a thing labeled as Christianity.

After I had been steeped in this type of Christian understanding for eighteen years, it makes sense that my conscience was overworked and fragile by the time I showed up on campus at Concordia. As I was learning about the Lord's Supper, as understood by the ancient church, as preserved through confessional Lutheran thought, I started to want to believe it was true.

The more I read and researched the topic for class assignments, the more difficult it became to ignore. Not only that, I started to hear the Good News in it. It's like I was being illuminated and given new eyes with which to look at the topic. As I was losing my grip on faith in the teachings I'd always known, it was as if another, from outside of me, was grasping on to me. Holding me up and together. Keeping me. All based on truth claims. I started to feel cared for beyond the typical rhetoric from a reverend.

The way life shaped my inner voice hasn't been great. A lot

of people look within or listen within and hear a happy voice. They hear the voice of encouragement or of confidence. They naturally overcome struggles or insecurities with a self-led pep talk. Some are great with psyching themselves up to try new things and to take risks, to lift themselves back up after a disappointment or receiving bad news. They push themselves to speak up in public and to take up for themselves when they sense they are being taken advantage of. Volunteering at an outing to take the stage when called on in front of strangers. Things of that sort.

That was not my story as a younger man. I grew up with a mom who had schizophrenia and a dad who was on drugs and alcohol. I'm not sure which parent's condition impacted me in which ways, and I can't quite parse it out perfectly. What I do recall, however, is not knowing what to feel. My inner life was shot. The voice inside me was quiet, mostly, or negative. I suppose what I mean by my *inner life* or *inner voice* is my conscience. The thing inside you that lives with you and houses your thoughts and memories and interacts with them all. The part of you that knows you the most and engages you as you interact with people and the world around you. It even has a voice that sounds like you in your mind. You get it, right?

Sometimes, I think that growing up as a boy and having a mom who was schizophrenic took a unique toll on my childhood development. Because of her condition, she wasn't always fully present. Physically she was, but emotionally and otherwise she couldn't give of herself wholly to me or anyone, for that matter—though I give her undying credit for giving me all she could give of herself.

Once I was at the local community center across the street from my building in the Blumeyer public housing project. If you're from the hood in North St. Louis, you may know where that is.

Right before us kids were dismissed from the center's after-school program, I was called outside. I stepped out of the building and saw police and the ambulance. I was confused. Why am I seeing this? I looked around and saw my mom. She was being restrained and dragged into the back of an ambulance. I kept calling out to her and trying to stretch my little kid body as far as I could to be grabbed by her, but I couldn't overpower the adults who had a grip on me.

"Momma, momma!" I screamed.

"It's okay, Marcus. Your mom will be okay. We just have to take her to the hospital. She'll be okay. She'll be okay," they repeated.

I don't even remember who the person was that was talking to me. I noticed that my mom didn't seem to have any awareness of me, as if she wasn't herself. I do remember seeing a distant cousin who lived in the neighborhood, but that's about it. I was so distraught by the sight of seeing my mom being taken away from me against her will that I broke out into hives all over my body from stress. Up until then, I thought my mom was like all the other moms. That's my first memory of discovering that my mom was different.

Though I had not seen what events led up to the situation or witnessed any of her behavior, I found out that day that something was wrong. Little did I know, that was only the tip of the iceberg. In front of me would be her entire life span of schizophrenic episodes. Visits to psychiatric centers and numerous occasions of trying to figure out what psych medications would best help her cope with her condition.

Terrible episodes ensued because of that struggle, not to mention bad theology telling her that God would heal her *if*. If this, if that. Just do this or that, and God will heal you. That was a constant battle for our entire household—my dad, my mom, and I. One moment, she would be doing fairly well on her medications, and then all of a sudden, she would hear some preacher on TV or visit some nearby church, and they would tell her to trust God and stop taking her medicine. They insisted that medication was a sign of a lack of faith, that demons could get in her body and soul through the meds and that she needed to fully trust God to heal her mind, not "man's cure."

Back and forth, back and forth. For this reason and a few others, I grew up not always feeling like the child. I also grew up without a healthy attachment or emotional bond to my parents. The good thing is, as a kid, you're not aware of these things and manage to find a way to keep trucking. Thanks to my dear grandmother, Frances Jones, I was blessed to bond with her like a mom. I was also blessed to have my wonderful family filled with aunts, uncles, grandparents, and cousins who filled my heart with endless love and laughs and distracted me from the sometimes horrors of home life. I am grateful that my parents did the best they could with what life dealt them and their baby boy, who they had to raise as young parents.

I had a notebook of raps and prayers. In it, I remember asking God to help me feel, begging Him to give me emotional sensory on the inside. There were times when it was appropriate to cry, but I couldn't bring myself to feel sad. Moments when it was right to be afraid, but I felt no fear or anything. Circumstances set for celebration, and I struggled to strum up excitement. Most of the time, I was coasting along in neutral. This indeed put a strain on my friendships growing up. Some chalked it up to me being selfish or weird. Perhaps that was true in the sense that we all are sinners, but in another sense, I simply was void of certain natural responses that others took for granted.

It all makes sense now; I was produced in expressions of Christianity that asked me to look within myself too often.

During my days in the Full Gospel Baptist denomination, it was emphasized and required that one learns to discern the voice of God from within. *That little, still, small, quiet voice*, they would say. *That is how God speaks*, they would explain. *If you meditate on God's Word long enough and live a life of obedience, then God will grant you greater measures of spiritual discernment and capabilities to notice when He is talking to you.* Who wouldn't want that gift?

This was a tall order for someone like myself, who suffered through the silence and distance of a schizophrenic mom. I was depleted and empty on the inside in many respects due to the nature of my household and childhood development, raised by a dear woman who, at times, would not even recognize me. Or worse, at times, would think I was Satan sent to attack her. Therefore, she would strike to attack me. Convinced sometimes that both my dad and I were out to harm her. We would both have to patiently love her through those episodes until her spirit would calm down.

Couple this with living with my beloved dad, who had his bouts with drugs and alcoholism. In and out of the house. Coming home drunk and high, sometimes in a violent rage. Getting into loud arguments with my mom with little to no good reason for being away from home for days. Leaving her alone for decent stretches of time to care for me when she was struggling to care for herself.

I recall the time my dad called home one day around 3:00 a.m. He dragged himself to a payphone from a nearby alleyway. He had been in an altercation with a police officer and a drug dealer that left both sides of his ribs cracked. I picked up the phone and heard him crying and begging for help. It was a traumatic thing to hear as his son. Truly. This altercation landed him in an alternative-to-prison program for three years. He was court ordered to leave home and move into a facility to satisfy the courts and to get help with his drug and alcohol addictions.

In many ways, I felt like a parent. I didn't feel prepared or equipped for that responsibility. I was missing a lot on the inside. I didn't feel I had the emotional resources to make the types of choices that needed to be made in the adult world. But I tried my best. Meanwhile, Christianity was in the backdrop, but the version of Christianity that was making me listen within to hear from God. Listen within to hear from God? Sheesh! I don't even know how to listen within to discern if I like myself or not. My "within" and inner sanctum was darkened and wasn't always a friendly place for my spirit to dwell. So therefore, why would God choose to speak to me in there?

From there I got introduced to another style of Christian existence: Reformed thought. Calvinism, in many ways, was a step in the right direction. It helped me shrink my unnatural appetite for the spiritual experiences that I had been chasing down at conferences and revivals, itching for the next spiritual high. I was less desperate for God to display a miracle in our midst. I scaled back my drive to perform more radical spiritual exploits to show God how good I had gotten with hearing His voice—even giving people "a word from God" that proved to be false and not a word from God.

Let's back up a minute. Under my previous thinking, there had been a time I thought God was giving me a sign to purchase a new truck—a Ford F-150. I believed I was getting "confirmation" from all over the place: billboards, random commercials advertising the truck, and my inner voice saying, *Yes, claim your truck in Jesus' name.* I even went to the dealership one night to lay hands on the truck to claim it in the name of Jesus. This was commonplace in the church circle I was brought up in—the Christian's version of the "manifestation" and "affirmation" craze popular these days.

Eventually, I went back up to the dealership to get the truck but was denied due to having no credit. I eventually attained a cosigner and was able to get the truck. I was struggling each month to make payments, payments totaling $745 dollars per month, at eighteen years old. After my missing payments for so long, it was eventually repossessed. That still didn't get me off the hook. I remained responsible for paying for the truck even after they came and got it. What a nightmare. All because I thought God spoke to me and gave me the green light to make the purchase, coupled with a collection of "confirmations." I was wrong.

I even told a friend of mine that God had told me to tell him—because I thought I heard God say so—that if he would come to Jesus that he would be blessed with a new Ford Mustang. I said to him, "My God owns everything, even cattle on a thousand hills," quoting Psalm 50:10–11: "For every beast of the forest is Mine, the cattle on a thousand hills. I know all the birds of the hills, and all that moves in the field is Mine."

My friend really wanted that Mustang and thought, *Well, this sounds easy. Just give my life to Jesus and get a new car? Say less!* He, too, went to the dealership and got denied. He made his way back to me and expressed his disappointment with the Christian God who couldn't even get him a new car. That day he turned away from the Lord. Forgive me, Lord.

It was moving away from that type of thinking that Calvinism helped me with. Struggling with assurance of salvation was not a common concern in the Full Gospel Baptist circle, or at least not thought about with that term. The struggle there was with "losing your anointing," meaning God anoints some uniquely with favor. Typically, this favor is earned and maintained by living a holy lifestyle, staying humble, and helping people. Added to that would be good-to-perfect attendance in church services and sharing Jesus with strangers everywhere you go. Do those things and get marked as one of the good Christians. One of the special ones. The anointed or chosen child.

The thought is taken from Luke 2:52: "And Jesus increased in . . . favor with God and man."

Mistakenly, the thinking goes, if we ought to be like Jesus, then surely we can grow in favor with God and man too, as if Luke 2:52 were a formula for getting ahead in life and in God's kingdom. It is not. Through Calvinism, I received a healthier understanding about which way to orient my life and decision-making: not based on seeking an inner voice or a supernatural experience but from knowing God more through His Word. That was good for me to hear, because it started my journey of thinking more about my faith, knowing more about what I believed and why I believed it.

I was exposed to the Reformation, to many dynamic preachers, and to those Calvinist reformers called the Puritans. As I was taking in heavy doses of Reformed Baptist thought, I was loving it! I made a lot of new friends and acquaintances who shared some of my experiences. Most of them had been brought up in the Charismatic church also. As young pupils of Calvinism, we were all taught the TULIP. Admittedly, most people struggle with limited atonement. This is why you have those known as four-point Calvinists because they cannot bring themselves to confessing a limitation on the atonement. To them, I say amen. Way to hang on to biblical fidelity amid the pressure to follow the logical order of the acronym.

However, I was not one them. I went all in! A staunch five-point Calvinist. Along with embracing limited atonement, I embraced double predestination, unfortunately. These would prove to be the two planks that would float me frantically backward to a more inward focus, a dependence on my inner voice and on the quality of my inner life. I was called to monitor my motives. *Why are you doing this good deed, Marcus? For acceptance or for God's glory?* I was called to have religious affections purely set on the kind God has. *Therefore, make sure you are joyful as close to all the time as humanly possible. You must fight for joy because God is joyful.* I must be killing sin in my heart in the most meticulous way, not mere behavior modification only. *Even non-Christians can do that*, it would be said. *Your change must look different, showing what Holy Spirit–borne fruit looks like compared to worldly moral improvement.*

Eventually, it started to feel like I had made a lateral move and not one for the better. Just different. There I was again, caught in a camp asking me to centralize my inner life in such a way that I would get some positive result from God. Things beyond simple trust that Jesus saves and sustains through Word and Sacrament. Not that, but an intentional focus on my inner man for the sake of signaling something to God in order to earn or keep something I thought He gave to the church freely.

I was wondering if I was one of the chosen Jesus actually died for, fearing that God potentially created me for hell (double predestination) and being haunted by Matthew 7:21–23:

> **Not everyone who says to Me, "Lord, Lord," will enter the kingdom of heaven, but the one who does the will of My Father who is in heaven. On that day many will say to Me, "Lord, Lord, did we not proph-**

> esy in Your name, and cast out demons in Your name, and do many mighty works in Your name?" And then will I declare to them, "I never knew you; depart from Me, you workers of lawlessness."

I found myself back in spiritual drought. A dry, weary, and desperate place. I say it like this in my song "Scattered Tulips" from my *Extra Nos* project:

> *Verse 1*
>
> *Hollin' / Hollin' / Hallelujah God / It came in the nick of time / Calvinism was sublime / Rescued me from my decline / Bigger picture painted God / Scripture gets prioritized / Plus it fit my introverted nerdy burdened quirky side / I'm persuaded by the Bible Mr. John / Sold his exegesis from Geneva, Switzerland / But it's crazy though / You put what you know / To the fire / Test your systematics with other erudite paradigms (what you find?) / You find great men / Who know Greek Hebrew too / You find great women well learned outside of group / Then them strong pillars that used to stand start to fall / Now you're diggin' through the rubble struggle to rebuild your walls (hold up).*
>
> *Hook*

I see scattered tulips / Come with me I show you what I found / I be diggin' in the text / Funny what you find when you're low to the ground. (repeat)

Verse 2

Hollin' / Hollin' / I can't take it God / Now I need some peace of mind / Tulips seen on the ground they eisegeted Romans 9 / From what used to seem like the biggest thing at the time / God's sovereignty / Started really shrinking God down in size / I'm predestined, right / Let's assume I'm one of the elect / At a low point / Life a mess in the flesh / Where you find me at / Introspecting trying to check / Looking deep within myself trying my best to assess / Was I genuine / Am I regenerate / Better yet / Was I ever really with Him / Will He hit me with Matthew 7 / Let's be clear / We justified by our faith / Maybe Mr. Calvin had sanctification out of place / I don't know.

Hook

This song means a great deal to me. It's one of my all-time personal favorites, not in a boastful way but because it articulates my inner struggle in theological terms. It expresses my psychological learning with my theological training at the time. It highlights the problems my personality had to bear when I was focusing so much on myself, my growth, my personal improvement. I struggled as an adult to be the type of person I was never granted the opportunity to become—the kind of person who can depend on something inside himself—to help pick myself up and feel the right things and do the right things.

Right alongside of being taught the theology of the TULIP, I wish I would have been able to also consider and compare what each one of those doctrines would have done for my personal growth and development. When I showed up on Concordia's doorstep, I was severely fractured. I suppose someone can read this and think I'm being extreme or that I had a personal vendetta with the Reformed. I assure you, I did not. This was simply my personal experience. Not only mine but so many others. They may not have written a book on it or composed music about its effects, but they have shared their stories with me and others. I've sat with them and had conversations for hours. I've read their emails and direct messages. I've spoken to so many over the phone and heard their stories. I've met many at concerts, where we chatted for long periods of time after the show. In addition, I have also met many who have communicated about these experiences: books, articles, and even podcast episodes on what it's like to survive such a culture of theological ideas.

The Lord's Supper Among the Fathers

One of the most comforting things for me when studying at Concordia (and continuously) was realizing that the Lutheran fathers were not inventing strange ideas or grabbing them out of thin air. Quite the opposite, in fact. They were among the believers who sought to reach back into church history to make sure the things they were teaching are rooted in Scripture and in the church fathers. Dr. Luther was careful to quote the apostolic fathers and early church fathers alike, in context, to demonstrate the origins of his rhetoric, being careful to only affirm what he found consistent with the Bible and the Creeds as preserved in the teachings of the disciples.

Realizing that the church held to the truth of the real presence long before the teaching of a metaphorical or symbolic view of the Lord's Supper was a game changer for me. It helped relax my skepticism and built in me a trust of the ancient interpretation. One of the principles emphasized in the Reformed camp was *sola Scriptura*, Scripture alone. Borrowing from Martin Luther, John Calvin agreed and echoed the emphasis. Because of this principle, I knew that if I were to embrace a teaching, it must ultimately be rooted in the Word of God and not contradict it.

That was a helpful principle to learn because it helped me look to the Scriptures to show that Jesus meant what He said when He used the word *is* concerning the Supper. After reexamining them, I saw that is exactly what the Bible teaches. Alongside that, Lutherans also teach healthily that having Scripture as the final authority does not at all mean that tradition has no place or any authority. That is important to keep in mind because the church gets her understanding of the faith from good, godly saints who preserved the teaching of Christianity and passed it down from the apostles.

Does tradition trump the Word of God? No. Does tradition stand over the Bible as a dictator? Not at all. Yet it is helpful to consider how the church has thought about and interpreted Scripture in those early years. In the context of this book, it is helpful to see how the church understood the Sacraments. This is not to say that there is perfect agreement in every little thing among the early church fathers and their writings. There certainly are differences, both subtle nuances and strong points of disagreement on certain matters between those early teachers of the church. Yet this is not the case concerning baptismal regeneration or the nature of the Lord's Supper.

There is an airtight unity among the church fathers related to God's work in Baptism and Jesus' bodily presence in the bread and the wine. I do not understand how a reader can visit the works of the earliest writings of the church fathers and come away with any other understanding than the mystical union taking place between God and people in the Sacraments. It is genuinely all over the place. Indeed, this consensus is preserved among the church with the claim of receiving the teachings directly from the apostles, who got them from Jesus Himself.

For two years, during my studies, I was immersed in the Book of Concord, the Lutheran Confessions, and I constantly noticed the insistent references to the church fathers. As I read them, I kept thinking to myself, *Wow, the church has believed these things, this way, since her origin? How did I miss this? Why was I not taught this?* Driven by that emotion, I was moved to look up a few of these persons and their writings to determine for myself if these words were actually there. As I did, I could not deny the primary sources, some of which I've shared below.

Tertullian on Communion

The flesh, indeed, is washed, in order that the soul may be cleansed; the flesh is anointed, that the soul may be consecrated; the flesh is signed (with the cross), that the soul too may be fortified; the flesh

> **is shadowed with the imposition of hands, that the soul also maybe illuminated by the Spirit; the flesh feeds on the body and blood of Christ, that the soul likewise may fatten on its God.**[41]

Here we see how Tertullian took to heart that "the flesh" (our body) and our soul, as they participate in Baptism and the Lord's Supper, receive the fullness of God, in Christ Jesus, not merely a symbolic reenactment of past events performed by Jesus.

> **Then, having taken the bread and given it to His disciples, He made it His own body, by saying, "This is my body," that is, the figure of my body. A figure, however, there could not have been, unless there were first a veritable body.**[42]

As I read these words, I started to see how normal it was for the church to think this way. They were not distracted by the "weirdness" of it all. Nor did they, who may have had an excuse given the prominence of philosophy in their day, resist on the grounds of "This is irrational and impossible, therefore, we cannot believe it." No, they said to themselves, "If Jesus said it, amen." I love how Tertullian phrases it here. He says, "He made it His own body, by saying, 'This is my body.'" Wow! Sounds like the opening words of the Bible in Genesis 1:3: "And God said, 'Let there be light,' and there was light."

I notice a natural desire among us Christians to long for the supernatural and to yearn for an encounter with God. Amen. Oftentimes, that good and holy desire gets fed with the wrong things, however. People so easily go after a popular personality promising

41 Tertullian, *On the Resurrection of the Flesh*, chapter 8 (*ANF* 3:551).

42 Tertullian, *The Five Books Against Marcion*, Book 4, chapter 40 (*ANF* 3:418).

to perform miracles, chasing down a prophecy, hoping to hear a personal word from God. While all along, the miraculous and supernatural encounter with God has already been provided for by God. Yes, God Himself is present in the sacramental elements supernaturally, mystically, with the sole purpose of delivering Himself to us. The Word in the most personal form. The ultimate gift, supplying us with everything we could ever truly need in this body-and-soul existence.

Cyprian of Carthage on Communion

These words, written with such tender affection, proved to me how precious and useful the early saints found the Lord's Supper in daily life as a believer in Christ, our Lord:

> And we ask that this bread should be given to us daily, that we who are in Christ, and daily receive the Eucharist for the food of salvation, may not, by the interposition of some heinous sin, by being prevented, as withheld and not communicating, from partaking of the heavenly bread, be separated from Christ's body, as He Himself predicts and warns, "I am the bread of life which came down from heaven. If any man eat of my bread, he shall live for ever: and the bread which I will give is my flesh, for the life of the world." . . . Therefore we ask that our bread—that is, Christ—may be given to us daily, that we who abide and live in Christ may not depart from His sanctification and body.[43]

One of the things I love about Cyprian is how he rightly weaves

43 *The Treatises of Cyprian*, Treatise 4, paragraph 18 (*ANF* 5:452).

the Sacraments into regular Christian affairs. Not by any stretch of the imagination is the Lord's Table an afterthought or a thing relegated to the outside, only to be discussed every now and again. He understands that the lifeline of the church is Christ Jesus, that Christ Himself implemented the Lord's Supper to nourish us and to unite us as His Body. He speaks of the Eucharist as protection from danger against our adversary and the foolishness of denying Christ's body and blood in the Meal.

Certainly noteworthy is his treatise on the unity of the church. He understands that the Communion meal is meant to unite the brothers and sisters in the faith to one another, in Christ. In the Meal, God preserves our unity by the power of His Spirit. He sustains our faith, which causes us to prioritize unity among one another.

Augustine of Hippo on Communion

> **That bread which you see on the altar, sanctified by the word of God, is the body of Christ. That cup, or rather what the cup contains, sanctified by the word of God, is the blood of Christ. It was by means of these things that the Lord Christ wished to present us with his body and blood, which he shed for our sake for the forgiveness of sins.[44]**
>
> **The Lord Jesus wished himself to be recognized in the breaking of bread, by those whose eyes had been kept till then from recognizing him. The faithful know what I'm talking about; they know Christ in the breaking of bread. It isn't every loaf of bread,**

44 Augustine, *Sermones ad Populum*, Sermon 227.

> you see, but the one receiving Christ's blessing, that becomes the body of Christ.[45]
>
> What you can see, then, is bread and a cup; that's what even your eyes tell you; but as for what your faith asks to be instructed about, the bread is the body of Christ, the cup the blood of Christ.[46]

St. Augustine uses strong and intentional language to describe the eucharistic mystery in a way that cannot be mistaken as an empty representation of what Jesus did a long time ago.

Irenaeus of Lyons on Communion

> But how can they be consistent with themselves, [when they say] that the bread over which thanks have been given is the body of their Lord and the cup His blood, if they do not call Himself the Son of the Creator of the world. . . . How can they say that the flesh, which is nourished with the body of the Lord and with His blood, goes to corruption, and does not partake of life? . . . For as the bread, which is produced from the earth, when it receives the invocation of God, is no longer common bread, but the Eucharist, consisting of two realities, earthly and heavenly; so also our bodies, when they receive the Eucharist, are no longer corruptible, having the hope of the resurrection to eternity.[47]

45 Augustine, *Sermons on the Liturgical Seasons*, Sermon 234:2.

46 Augustine, *Sermons on the Liturgical Seasons*, Sermon 272.

47 Irenaeus, *Against Heresies*, Book 4, chapter 18, paragraph 4 (*ANF* 1:486). Brackets in original.

> **But if this indeed do [*sic*] not attain salvation, then neither did the Lord redeem us with His blood, nor is the cup of the Eucharist the communion of His blood, nor the bread which we break the communion of His body. . . . He has acknowledged the cup (which is a part of the creation) as His own blood, from which He bedews our blood; and the bread (also a part of the creation) He has established as His own body, from which He gives increase to our bodies.**
>
> **When, therefore, the mingled cup and the manufactured bread receives the Word of God, and the Eucharist of the blood and the body of Christ is made, from which things the substance of our flesh is increased and supported, how can they affirm that the flesh is incapable of receiving the gift of God, which is life eternal, which [flesh] is nourished from the body and blood of the Lord?[48]**

Can our dear brother Irenaeus be more clear? He states plainly that the Eucharist, the Lord's Supper, is made up of the bread and wine as well as Jesus's body and blood. That is only part of the mystery: Irenaeus affirms that Jesus' body benefits our bodies, giving us life now and forever.

Justin Martyr on Communion

> **And this food is called among us . . . [the Eucharist], of which no one is allowed to partake but the man**

48 Irenaeus, *Against Heresies*, Book 5, chapter 2, paragraphs 2–3 (*ANF* 1:528). Brackets in original.

> **who believes that the things which we teach are true, and who has been washed with the washing that is for the remission of sins, and unto regeneration, and who is so living as Christ has enjoined. For not as common bread and common drink do we receive these; but in like manner as Jesus Christ our Saviour, having been made flesh by the Word of God, had both flesh and blood for our salvation, so likewise have we been taught that the food which is blessed by the prayer of His word, and from which our blood and flesh by transmutation are nourished, is the flesh and blood of that Jesus who was made flesh.**[49]

Justin's words and the other writings of the early church fathers illustrate the importance and understanding of the Eucharist in early Christian theology. They reveal a belief in the real presence of Christ in the Sacrament and its significance for salvation, unity, and the anticipation of the resurrection.

It's like an entirely different world of Christianity, a different ethos where the Sacraments are not an afterthought but the core of the faith. All rooted in Jesus' Word and promises. Promises of forgiveness of sin and healing. Promises of protection and unity. Promises of assurance of salvation, immortality, and eternal life. There's a noticeable difference in how the early saints and those who follow after their heritage function.

Living in a pagan society in which life was cheap and morality was wild, Christians sought to define themselves by biblical confessions. Over against their deep connections to the culture of the Jews,

49 *The First Apology of Justin*, chapter 66 (*ANF* 1:185). Brackets in original.

they were learning to live the Christian way. To understand their identity in Christ and what it meant to live like such in the world. To weather the storms of persecution when they would blow. To ward off false teaching that sought to use elements of Christianity to deceive many. The theological teachers of the church had to wage war on the battlefield of ideas to protect the flock.

That type of environment produced some of the most Christ-centered writings and expositions of Scripture. The early saints were greatly informed about the centrality of Christ Jesus and His means to preserve His church. The teaching that the devil seemed to attack the most was the nature of Christ and the nature of salvation. For this reason, the early church fathers labored to defend the faith against attacks on the understanding of the nature of the Son of God. I find it curious that in doing so, they vehemently addressed the Lord's Supper and Baptism. The Lord's Supper was indeed a part of their apologetic, the defense of the faith. It further proved God's plan to save and sustain the church that He established in Christ.

A major priority was not only to defend the church against outside attacks but also to teach those inside the church what Christianity was so that families could learn and draw closer to their Lord through grace and knowledge. There was this through-line of life lived around the confessions of the apostles and those the apostles taught, resulting in writings that preserve such truths. Writings we find in the early creeds of the church.

If you are like me, you may feel like you've been a Christian for a lifetime and have never been exposed to creedal talk. *What are these creeds, Flame? What does the word* creed *even mean?* The word means "belief." A creed is basically a way of systematizing or organizing a set of beliefs. In this case, the beliefs are Christian ones. The ancient church confessed three mains creeds: the Apostles' Creed, the Nicene Creed, and the Athanasian Creed. They are called the three Ecumenical Creeds because they confess truths that the universal church adheres to. The word *ecumenical* means something related to the promotion of unity among a large group. Therefore, the goal of the Ecumenical Creeds is to provide a set of truths that can rightly define Christianity and cause Christians from all over the world to agree on that definition.

Even now, Christians from all over the world gather and recite these truths regularly during Sunday gatherings. It's extremely encouraging to think about. On any given Sunday, believers from near and far are verbally acknowledging that they confess the same thing as one another, all stemming from the teachings of the apostles themselves, who were taught by the Master Teacher Himself. Allow me to place them in this book for those who have never set eyes on these historical texts that unite us and have stood the test of time. I offer the Apostles' Creed below, and I include the other two (Nicene Creed and Athanasian Creed) in an appendix at the end of this book.

The Apostles' Creed (c. AD 341)

I believe in God, the Father Almighty, maker of heaven and earth.

And in Jesus Christ, His only Son, our Lord, who was conceived by the Holy Spirit, born of the virgin Mary, suffered under Pontius Pilate, was crucified,

> died, and was buried. He descended into hell. The third day He rose again from the dead. He ascended into heaven and sits on the right hand of God the Father Almighty. From thence He will come to judge the living and the dead.
>
> I believe in the Holy Spirit, the holy Christian Church, the communion of saints, the forgiveness of sins, the resurrection of the body, and the life everlasting. Amen.

When I read the Ecumenical Creeds and the goal therein, it reminds me of Jesus' High Priestly Prayer. Our dear Lord prays in John 17:14–22,

> I have given them Your word, and the world has hated them because they are not of the world, just as I am not of the world. I do not ask that You take them out of the world, but that You keep them from the evil one. They are not of the world, just as I am not of the world. Sanctify them in the truth; Your word is truth. As You sent Me into the world, so I have sent them into the world. And for their sake I consecrate Myself, that they also may be sanctified in truth. I do not ask for these only, but also for those who will believe in Me through their word, that they may all be one, just as You, Father, are in Me, and I in You, that they also may be in Us, so that the world may believe that You have sent Me. The glory that You have given Me I have given to them, that they may be one even as We are one.

What a dear and beautiful prayer of our Lord to His Father, recorded and documented for us to hear. To recite even. We can pray an exact pray from our Savior! Wow! From this prayer of our Lord, we see His concern for the truth, which is right teaching concerning Himself, the Second Person of the Trinity. We recognize a request for protection and sanctification performed by the truth, a focus on not only the disciples but also the entire church universal, including you reading this. Jesus prays, "I do not ask for these only, but also for those who will believe in Me through their word." Constantly, Jesus is praying for our unity. That we would be one. One as the Father and the Christ are one.

The early church fathers, as we have read, are always thinking about right doctrine, truth, and the unity of the church. That we would be one. A Christian culture set on the unity of the church is the utter opposite of the overall ethos of the generic American church. In our contemporary expression of the faith, we often get more focused on the individual rather than the whole. It is commonplace to find pop-Christian culture borrowing the language and mood of the surrounding culture and trying to Christianize common phrases.

"Becoming the best version of yourself" is one of those phrases. It is helpful to slow down sometimes and to consider what ideas we are embracing and forcing into our Christian mind. "Becoming the best version of yourself" is not a Christian concept, not what the teaching of sanctification is getting at. Spiritual growth is not about self. The worldly concept sets at the core the self, as if life is about fine-tuning your personal virtues, resulting in a "better you" or the "best you." Rather, the Christian life is about Jesus. It is about serving others in the many ways God has designed you to, as unto

Jesus. Loving others as we have been freely loved by Jesus. Growing more in our identity as the baptized—baptized into Christ Jesus.

A better way forward is to continue loving others as we love ourselves. This prevents us from becoming inward-focused or growing bitter toward people. We should remain near God's people as we all partake in Christ's body and blood through bread and wine, receiving the healing nourishment He promised. "Self-love" often has an isolated goal that doesn't offer the spiritually medicinal cure we might think it does. Isolation is not the goal of Christianity. Personal relationship is not the goal of Christianity. The "self" is not the goal of Christianity. The church fathers teach that we strive for unity in Christ.

Another expression of our misguided me-centered focus is our obsession with doing something for God, as opposed to resting in and living out of what He has done and is doing for us. This sometimes is a mask for our own desire for fame and attention, yet we coat it in language that sounds more spiritual, language like "Make God famous." Who taught us to say "Make God famous"? I've certainly said it many times. As if that is a good thing? As if that's something He asked us to do? Assuming that's something He would like, to merely be famous? Dumping on Him our lust and lowly goals for fame.

Please, do not make God famous. Instead, serve your neighbor well, as unto the Lord of glory. Quietly do good however you can with whatever resources God has entrusted to you. Trust that God uses the ordinary to impact deeply. His Holy Spirit is involved in those simple encounters and may be pleased to provide an opportunity for us to do more and share more. Share with the common person love, laughter, long-suffering, and forgiveness. Tell them about Jesus and the forgiveness of sins. To have their sins washed away in Baptism, by faith only, as we read in Acts 22:16:

> **And now why do you wait? Rise and be baptized and wash away your sins, calling on His name.**

CHAPTER 6

EYES WIDE OPEN

As I was learning more about the early church and how believers understood the Sacraments, I started to compare the things I gathered along the way with one another. During my time in the Full Gospel Baptist space, there was zero talk of the sacramental life. We would have Communion once every six months. It was taken seriously and treated with reverence as important, which I suppose is to be appreciated on some level. However, after that it, would fade back into obscurity and irrelevance. Mostly, you would only hear or think of Communion because it was being used in a comedy bit in a movie in some sacrilegious way.

In the Reformed world, there was little to no inclusion of the sacramental life mentioned. From the Reformed Baptist side of things, Communion was strictly considered a memorial occurrence, and that was it. I later learned that the Presbyterian and Anglican wings of the Calvinists do hold to a spiritual presence of Christ in the Supper but deny His bodily presence. I began to wonder why the different groups appeared to be so silent on the matter. There were several conferences where the Reformed would unite for the sake of the Gospel and understandably leave certain points of disagreement off the agenda. I get that.

They even shared several websites that featured blogs and articles related to culture and theology. Yet the Sacraments were not highlighted in a relevant way. I did listen to a debate between R. C. Sproul and John MacArthur on infant Baptism, but I found debate buried in a box at a conference. It did not occupy prime real estate among the other merchandise offered. Beyond that, you probably would have only known about the differences if you came from another theological background such as Roman Catholicism, Lutheranism, or the Eastern Orthodox Church.

I struggled to understand how things shifted so dramatically. From what I was discovering, the Sacraments held primacy in life and doctrine among the early church. Whenever the church fathers would pick up the pen, so to speak, they couldn't help but to include these mysteries. Even the church's detractors understood that the Sacraments were a way of life for the small sect.

I gathered that if the Reformed from different camps could keep so quiet about their disagreements among one another, then their silence screamed of what place they gave the rites among their ranks. They relegated them to ceremonies that mean a great deal but don't need to be front and center, at least not as much as the Gospel. That to me is a clear confession in and of itself. Functionally, the Sacraments are not held as the Gospel but as a sacred component related to it at best or a work of man at worst.

Either way, the placement of the Sacraments was clearly moved into the distance. That much started to become apparent. This is something most Protestants have done, unfortunately. Rarely would I hear talk of creeds or confessions. I knew about the 1689 Baptist Confession, but it wasn't drawn on in any real way among the Reformed Baptist. The Presbyterians, however, were more known for referencing the Westminster Confession of Faith; I give them that. I knew nothing of the Anglicans at the time. Still, it was becoming more clear to me that Christianity had taken on a different shape, and that shape was not fitted for a life formed to sacramental size.

As I began to dig deeper into this matter, I recognized the clear departure. The Protestants read much differently than the ancient church compared to the confessional Lutherans. As a staunch five-point Calvinist at the time, being as unbiased as I could possibly be, I saw how differently the Reformed Baptists taught the Supper than the church fathers. Even John Calvin himself would disagree with the Reformed Baptists and other Protestants.

Read for yourself the differences in understanding concerning the Sacrament of the Altar. You'll be able to see the stark distinctions between the ancient church's teaching versus that of the Baptists and the Reformed. Then you'll notice the confessional Lutherans' voice simply trying to echo the voice of the fathers. To be sure, this is not a petty contest to say, "Look at us. We're better or more right." Not at all. I get zero joy from that and gain absolutely nothing by it.

The sole purpose of this comparison is to highlight the hope the Sacrament offers as a provision for the church, her salvation, and her unity. When the mystical union is removed, it falls short of Jesus' original intent. Even as John Calvin seeks to find a middle ground between his two predecessors Ulrich Zwingli and Martin Luther, he still walks away with less than what the ancient church taught and what the apostles themselves taught.

Below, I am including quotes for comparison, and the order flows as follows: the early church (1), the Reformed Baptists (2), the Calvinists (3), the confessional Lutherans (4). Repeat. A few times, I alternate between the Westminster Confession of Faith and a direct quote from John Calvin to represent the Reformed view of the Supper. Make note of similarities and differences.

1. Ignatius of Antioch (Early Church)

I have no delight in corruptible food, nor in the pleasures of this life. I desire the bread of God, the heavenly bread, the bread of life, which is the flesh of Jesus Christ, the Son of God, who became afterwards of the seed of David and Abraham; and I desire the drink, namely His blood, which is incorruptible love and eternal life.[50]

They [the Gnostics] abstain from the Eucharist and from prayer because they confess not the Eucharist to be the flesh of our Saviour Jesus Christ, which suffered for our sins, and which the Father, of His goodness, raised up again.[51]

2. 1689 Baptist Confession of Faith (Reformed Baptists)

The supper of the Lord Jesus was instituted by him the same night wherein he was betrayed, to be observed in his churches, unto the end of the world, for the perpetual remembrance, and showing to all the world the sacrifice of himself in his death, confirmation of the faith of believers in all the benefits thereof, their spiritual nourishment, and growth in him, their further engagement in, and to all duties which they owe to him; and to be a bond and pledge of their communion with him, and with each other.

50 *Epistle of Ignatius to the Romans*, chapter 7 (*ANF* 1:77).
51 *Epistle of Ignatius to the Smyrnaeans*, chapter 7 (*ANF* 1:89).

. . . But only a memorial of that one offering up of himself by himself upon the cross.[52]

3. Westminster Confession of Faith (Calvinists)

The outward elements in this Sacrament, duly set apart to the uses ordained by Christ, have such relation to him crucified, as that truly, yet sacramentally only, they are sometimes called by the name of the things they represent, to wit, the body and blood of Christ.[53]

4. Large Catechism (Confessional Lutherans)

"Now, what is the Sacrament of the Altar?"

Answer, "It is the true body and blood of our Lord Jesus Christ, in and under the bread and wine, which we Christians are commanded by Christ's Word to eat and to drink." Just as we have said that Baptism is not simple water, so here also we say that though the Sacrament is bread and wine, it is not mere bread and wine, such as are ordinarily served at the table [1 Corinthians 10:16–17]. But this is bread and wine included in, and connected with, God's Word.[54]

---

52 The 1689 Baptist Confession of Faith, chapter 30, paragraphs 1 and 2, accessed December 23, 2024, https://www.the1689confession.com/1689/chapter-30.

53 The Westminster Confession of Faith, chapter 29, section 5 (T. & T. Clark, 1881), 155–56.

54 Large Catechism, Part 5, paragraphs 8–9. Brackets in original.

1. St. Clement of Alexandria (Early Church)

> And calling her children to her, she nurses them with holy milk, viz., with the Word for childhood. . . . The Word is all to the child, both father and mother and tutor and nurse. "Eat ye my flesh," He says, "and drink my blood." Such is the suitable food which the Lord ministers, and He offers His flesh and pours forth His blood, and nothing is wanting for the children's growth. O amazing mystery![55]

2. 1689 Baptist Confession of Faith (Reformed Baptists)

> Worthy receivers, outwardly partaking of the visible elements in this ordinance, do then also inwardly by faith, really and indeed, yet not carnally and corporally, but spiritually receive, and feed upon Christ crucified, and all the benefits of His death; the body and blood of Christ being then not corporally or carnally, but spiritually present to the faith of believers in that ordinance, as the elements themselves are to their outward senses.[56]

55 Clement of Alexandria, *The Instructor*, Book 1, chapter 6 (*ANF* 2:220).

56 The 1689 Baptist Confession of Faith, chapter 30, paragraph 7.

3. John Calvin's *Institutes* (Calvinists)

> So, when bread is given to us as a symbol of the body of Christ, we ought immediately grasp this comparison, that, as bread nourishes, sustains, and preserves the life of the body, so the body of Christ is the only food to animate and support the life of the soul. When we see wine presented as a symbol of his blood, we ought to think of the uses wine imparts to the human body, that we may contemplate the same advantages conferred upon us in a spiritual manner by the blood of Christ.[57]

4. Large Catechism (Confessional Lutherans)

> It is the Word, I say, which makes and sets this Sacrament apart. So it is not mere bread and wine, but is, and is called, Christ's body and blood [1 Corinthians 11:23–27]. For it is said, "When the Word is joined to the element or natural substance, it becomes a Sacrament." This saying of St. Augustine is so properly and so well put that he has scarcely said anything better. The Word must make a Sacrament out of the element, or else it remains a mere element.[58]

57 John Calvin, *Institutes of the Christian Religion*, vol. 2, Book 4, chapter 17 (Presbyterian Board of Publication, 1909), 643–44.

58 Large Catechism, Part 5, paragraph 10. Brackets in original.

1. Origen (Early Church)

> But now, "in reality," the flesh of the Word of God is "true food," just as he himself says: "My flesh is truly food, and my blood is truly drink."[59]

2. 1689 Baptist Confession of Faith (Reformed Baptists)

> The outward elements in this ordinance, duly set apart to the use ordained by Christ, have such relation to him crucified, as that truly, although in terms used figuratively, they are sometimes called by the names of the things they represent, in other words, the body and blood of Christ, albeit, in substance and nature, they still remain truly and only bread and wine, as they were before.[60]

3. John Calvin's *Institutes* (Calvinists)

> Only I reject the absurdities which appear to be either degrading to his majesty, or inconsistent with the reality of his human nature, and are at the same time repugnant to the word of God, which informs us that Christ has been received into the glory of the celestial kingdom, where he is exalted above every condition of the world, and which is equally careful to attribute his human nature the properties of real humanity.[61]

59 Origen, *Homilies on Numbers*, Book 2, chapter 7 (Ancient Christian Texts, ed. Christopher A. Hall, trans. Thomas P. Scheck [IVP Academic Press, 2009], 26–27).

60 The 1689 Baptist Confession of Faith, chapter 30, paragraph 5.

61 Calvin, *Institutes*, 684–85.

4. Large Catechism (Confessional Lutherans)

With this Word, you can strengthen your conscience and say: "If a hundred thousand devils, together with all fanatics, should rush forward, crying, 'How can bread and wine be Christ's body and blood?' and such, I know that all spirits and scholars together are not as wise as the Divine Majesty in His little finger" [see 1 Corinthians 1:25]. Now here stands Christ's Word: "Take, eat; this is My body. . . . Drink of it, all of you; this is My blood of the new testament," and so on. Here we stop to watch those who will call themselves His masters and make the matter different from what He has spoken. It is true indeed, that if you take away the Word or regard the Sacrament without the words, you have nothing but mere bread and wine. But if the words remain with them, as they shall and must, then, by virtue of the words, it is truly Christ's body and blood.[62]

62 Large Catechism, Part 5, paragraphs 12–14. Brackets in original.

I hope by now you're seeing the major differences between how the early church rightly understood the Sacraments compared to what Reformed teachings later became and how the confessional Lutherans simply fought to preserve what the church has always confessed since the beginning.

Interesting, huh? If you're anything like I was, you're blown away by this! It's remarkable. It's new information. It can even be a bit alarming. Don't panic, though. Christianity is still trustworthy despite this major shift in understanding here. As you continue to read, you'll get a better understanding of how this shift happened, specifically in the West and in the Americas. Just keep reading. What I'm also hoping you notice is the utter hope and power the early church and the Lutherans draw from the Meal Jesus instituted. There's an utter abandonment of any limits placed on God and what He can or cannot do. As if we could set the rules and standard for Him to abide by. Not at all.

I'm reminded of two lyrics from my EP *Christ for You* that discuss the Lord's Supper. One from "Sounds Crazy" says,

> ***So we gone take God made physics / And try to keep Christ in those limits / Consider we call ourselves Christian / And visit the Scriptures / And see it's filled with it / Ample examples of instances / Ok let's see if you remember this / Remember on the road with Cleopas / After Christ rose then He strolled to Emmaus / At the table took bread broke it / He opened their eyes then He vanished /***

Amazing / He physically disappeared / What He does with His body to us is weird / But His personal union / Divine and human natures should define why the church reveres / A man who can walk on the water / Told Peter come walk on the water / Plus He made wine out of water / Baptized us in the water / And He healed Jairus's daughter / Now all of a sudden we doubt the author / Zwingli then Calvin's sentiment / "The finite's not capable of the infinite" / In that case then this central incident / Called the incarnation is not legit.

And the other one, from "That Long," says,

And Calvin started placing his limits / On Jesus' metaphysics (in the Institutes) / And lead with his presuppositions / And keeping them over the Scriptures, facts.

I assure you, I am not simply "quote mining" above, grabbing random quotes and taking them out of context to prove my point. To avoid such accusations, I have cited sources. You can search the internet for plenty of free resources and fact-check me. You can also read them in their immediate and full context and see that they all hold in the same way I am using them. What stands out to me is John Calvin's disdain for the very thought of Jesus being bodily present in the bread and wine. He says quite bluntly how he feels about anyone who takes Jesus at His Word that He is bodily present in the earthly elements:

> Nor will they find a man foolish enough to be persuaded to believe so an absurdity. . . . But it is essential to a real body, to have its particular form and dimensions, and to be contained within some certain space. Let us bear no more, then, of this ridiculous notion, which fastens the minds of men, and Christ himself, to the bread.[63]

Respectfully, this speaks to his misunderstanding of the nature of Christ Jesus.

He goes on to further describe how Christ's body is limited by the metaphysics He created and cannot do certain things in His own creation. He then poses a more rational and plausible explanation:

> They allege that Christ came out of the sepulchre, while the sepulchre remained closed, and entered into the room where his disciples were assembled, while the doors were shut; but this contributes no support to their error. For as the water was like a solid pavement, forming a road for Christ when he walked on the lake, so it is no wonder if the hardness of the stone gave way, to make him a passage; though it is more probable that the stone removed at his command, and after his departure returned to its place.[64]

63 Calvin, *Institutes*, 680–81.

64 Calvin, *Institutes*, 681.

See, it is easier for him to drum up a more reasonable explanation for Jesus and Peter walking on water. The water must have taken on the form of a "solid pavement." We might picture ice in our language and context.

Yet for St. Gregory of Nyssa, he doesn't doubt the mystery but acknowledges what Jesus reveals to be exactly what He said. For He is the Word Himself become flesh:

> **By dispensation of His grace, He spreads Himself in every believer through that flesh, whose substance comes from wine and bread, blending Himself with the bodies of believers, to secure that, by this union with the immortal, man, too, may be a sharer in incorruption.**[65]

I address the confusion concerning Christ's nature in a song titled "3 Genera":

> ***Verse 1***
>
> ***Examine it church / We learned that concerning the person of Christ / That Calvin is close / But Lutherans know / That we get it right / Talking about how His attributes / Communicate with other attributes / I mean His divinity and His humanity / Let's just call it the three genera / Never catch me saying gang gang / But genus genera / Them Latin words / That simply means k-i-n-d / A sharing***

65 Gregory of Nyssa, *The Great Catechism*, chapter 37 (*NPNF2* 5:506).

between / Christ's natures to person / First genus IDIOMATICUM / Idioma just means "attribute" / The human nature / The divine nature / both communicating contributions to / The One the Bible calls the Word / In possession of His two natures / Yes according to the divinity / He literally can be in two places / Both at the same time / The Son is considered descendent from David's line / According to human side / The night He was crucified / We can say God died.

Hook

Who, who do you say that I am (yeah) / That they denying My unity / Who, who do men say that I am (yeah) / That they got problems consuming Me / Who, who do men say that I am / Denying communication of My attributes / Who, who do men say that I am / Determining what My body can and cannot do / Who?

Verse 2

The second kind is MAIESTATICUM / That's just talking 'bout His majesty / The communication of divinity / That's received by His humanity / This how His body and blood / That's present in bread and the wine / Brings forgiveness through human nature / Receiving communication from the divine / That's why we confess with the Scriptures / And don't have an issue with reading it right / The Supper He instituted on that night is forgiving our sins and bringing us life / So when He's present at my table / Bodily present at y'all's table / Body present at 1,000 tables / Omnipresent body / God is able / This is how Jesus the man can be talked about as one that's giving us life / 'Cause that ain't what human beings do / Right? / Unless we're talking about Christ / The emphasis of MAIESTATICUM / Is what His divinity brings / To His human nature / Like divine power / His humanity only receives.

Hook

Verse 3

We in the thick of Christology / The third is APOTELESMATICUM / Apotelesma is a work /

And Jesus yeah He had a lot of them / Every work that the Word does / Both natures right there cuz / Cannot have one in heaven / One that made an exit / That's absurd cuz / The blood of Jesus yeah it purifies / Purifies us from all sin / You can find that in first John / 1 and 7 yeah He's all in / The act of this purification is from His blood / And that's His human nature / But the power to forgive is from divine nature / Both of them present in the Savior / Both natures / Every action / Sorry Calvin / No fraction / When miracles happen / Then the hypostatic union is in action / Like Christ's passion (no lacking) / He is forever the God-man / Let that settle in your heart / Cannot sever Him apart / Like two separate people nah / With His work.

Hook

When we think about us as humans, we sometimes try to stand over Jesus to tell Him what He's capable of doing, what He's not capable of doing. In reality, He's standing over us as our Head, and He's telling us, He's revealing to us what the truth is. He is the way. He is the truth and the life. So we do best to listen to Him. We do best to follow the Word of God and what it reveals and to not resist on the basis of "That feels weird" or "That sounds strange."

Those things may come naturally for us, those uncomfortable feelings or maybe a lack of familiarity with what's being said. Keep in mind that we're talking about what Jesus says.

I just want to give a shout-out to Dr. Leo Sanchez. It's so funny because I had to take a test about the nature of Christ, and I thought I killed it. I thought I killed it! I was like, "I know I aced this thing." And on every other portion of the test, I did. I killed it. But when it came to Christology, it was a little fuzzy, and my professor let me know. He pointed me to Dr. Sanchez.

The mental block there for me was the distinction between how at the time I as a Calvinist was processing Christology and contrasting that with the historic understanding of the nature of Christ, which goes all the way back to Cyril of Alexandria (and before), preserved through the confessional Lutheran tradition. That's what Dr. Sanchez did for me. He just walked me through things, and man, the Holy Spirit used that time. So, first, I just enjoyed that close proximity to him and being able to pick his brain because he's brilliant. He's genius. But then I was able just to learn more about my Lord. I was able to get into the Word of God. I was able to delve into theology even deeper just to see what God, through Christ, has done for us, all based upon Jesus' true nature. One person, two natures.

An article that is helpful in talking about the natures of Christ is "Christology Illustrated" by David R. Maxwell, which can be found in *Concordia Theology*. I highly encourage everyone to read it. I wish I could walk through it with you, line by line, but for now, I'll offer a basic summary of the three genera, leaning on the teachings of Dr. Maxwell.

I want to talk about the nature of Jesus and point out that this is important because it's tied to how we understand Jesus' words as they relate to the Sacraments. In terms of church history and the reformers who came after Martin Luther and his cohorts, part of the mental block with people like Zwingli and John Calvin and others was the way that they understood Jesus' nature. I would argue that, in an effort to sort of protect Jesus or to try to preserve something true about Jesus, they went to another extreme. So that's why this is essential to discuss; when we understand how Jesus exists, what He can do, and what He says He does with His own physical body, then we can better position ourselves to humble ourselves underneath His words and then just receive His gifts. So that's the dope thing about this conversation.

So anyway, let's get into Dr. Maxwell's teachings:

> **At the heart of Lutheran Christology lie the three *genera* of communication of attributes [or the three kinds of characteristics that Christ possesses]. . . . Therefore, when we speak of the three *genera* of communication of attributes, we are talking about three kinds of sharing that take place between Christ's natures and person. You can think of it as three different kinds of statements that the Scriptures make about Christ. Before we examine the three *genera*, we need to say a few words about how Lutheran Christology describes Christ.**[66]

Nestorius, who lived primarily in the fifth century, talks about Jesus' divine and human natures in a way that pretty much separates

66 David R. Maxwell, "Christology Illustrated (from the CT Vault)" *Concordia Theology*, January 19, 2011, https://concordiatheology.org/2011/01/christology-illustrated-from-the-ct-vault/ (accessed December 23, 2024).

Jesus as if He's two different people. The analogy is like two different wooden boards kind of stuck together. So there's not this oneness but two actual different people. That's not what the Bible says, so that's wrong. Lutherans hold to what Cyril of Alexandria taught, which is that Jesus is fully God and fully man all the time. In Jesus, there is no man that acts separately from God. Jesus is the Word made flesh with a human and divine nature.

All right, here we go. Think of Jesus as the Word. The first genus dealing with Jesus' attributes is that both His divine nature and His human nature communicate attributes to Him, the Word. From His divine nature, Jesus is all powerful, all knowing, all present, and so on. From His human nature, Jesus can grow, suffer, die, and so on. The phrase for this truth is *genus idiomaticum*, which means "the attribute kind." He's both God and man, and He has traits of both God and man. Bible passages such as 1 Corinthians 2:8 and Romans 1:3 talk about Jesus being both God and man at the same time. The Lord of glory can be crucified. The Son of God is also the Son of David.

Hopefully, you're seeing how these things are helpful in terms of categorizing and structuring the nature of Christ in your mind so far. We're dealing with the attributes of Jesus being God and man and how the Word shares in these two types of attributes based on His human and divine nature. Got it? Cool.

The next way Jesus' two natures interact is that His divine nature communicates divine attributes to His human nature but not the other way around. Dr. Maxwell calls this the *genus maiestaticum*, or "the majesty kind." For example, because Jesus is God, Jesus' body and blood have divine attributes. His blood is shed to forgive our sins. His body has divine power. But Jesus' divine nature doesn't become human. What is that all about? Let's find out. This is important when we talk about the Lord's Supper, because the Bible teaches that Christ's body and blood has power to forgive us and give us life. Jesus is able to forgive sin through His physical body and blood because the divine nature, or the majesty of God, is communicating this power, this reality, to His human nature. So as you're thinking, *Man, how can Jesus' body and blood provide forgiveness of sin?* then we ought to know it is according to the Son's divine majesty. The human nature is receiving something, not contributing anything back to the divine nature. The human nature is only receiving from the majesty of God, simply put, because human nature doesn't have the power or the ability to forgive sin or to give life. Got it? Good. Let's keep going.

Just walk with me, walk with me. So we have to keep this tight, and we're going with what the Scripture reveals. We're not going with logic or trying to find some kind of consistency according to our understanding. No, we're going with what God reveals, because that's what Christians do. So when we're talking about the Word having human attributes, that's according to the incarnation, Jesus becoming flesh. There's this sharing in humanity that God participates in. But we do not say that the divine nature has human attributes, because that would risk adding weakness to the divine nature. So what we see here again is that this genus protects the reality known from Scripture that the divinity is sending this power to humanity while the divinity does not receive any weakness back from the humanity. That's important. Keep that locked in mind.

Last one: the *genus apotelesmaticum* (the "final result," or "work"). According to this genus, "everything that Christ does, he does utilizing both natures. He never 'turns off' his divine nature."[67]

67 Maxwell, "Christology Illustrated."

As we know from John 6:51, Jesus has flesh, and He offers it to give life. Beautiful. Jesus has a body, and His body has divine power. Some would try to say that Jesus' body was not a part of His miraculous power, but that's separating His two natures too much. So that's the big point here: We're keeping all of these realities together. We're not denying things that are clear in the Bible. We're not affirming things that are not in the Bible. We're keeping this tight-knit. So every work that Jesus does, both natures are present in His work.

All three of these truths point to the unity of Christ:

1. Christ is the Word, with two natures, with divine and human attributes.
2. The divine and human natures have a close connection, with the divine nature giving divine attributes to the human nature, but not the other way around.
3. Both natures always work together with anything that Jesus does. This is essential when talking about salvation in Christ. God (divine) had to die (human) for us to be saved.

So we need the God-man to be the God-man so that we can actually have the forgiveness of sins from Him. Because if the God-man is just a man and not God, then that man is just like us. He can't provide forgiveness. That's what the *genus idiomaticum* helps us understand.

And how is it that we receive bread and wine and that as Jesus is bodily present in that bread and wine, our sins are being forgiven? It's because the divine nature is communicating that forgiving power to the human nature. And that's what we have going on when we're receiving the body and blood of our Lord. Beautiful.

Everything Jesus does, including His death and resurrection, uses both natures. Beautiful. And I love that because, again, I had come from the Reformed Baptist world, which didn't even understand these realities properly—so that they just made the Lord's Supper a symbol.

The Supper was just an empty symbol, a metaphor, a time to reflect on what Jesus did long ago, but nothing divine was happening. It wasn't heaven meeting earth and God communicating forgiveness and divine power to His human attributes so through body and blood in the elements we receive forgiveness. It wasn't that at all. But then there is an expression in the more Presbyterian expression of Calvinism, or the Reformed thought, in which Calvin made some type of middle ground between Zwingli and Luther—and this is why this conversation is important.

In Calvin's *Institutes*,[68] he first says that Jesus can't be bodily present in bread and wine. So he's separating the two natures in Jesus' work (*genus apotelesmaticum*). Calvin separates the work of the Word, saying that Christ's human nature is just sitting on the right hand of the Father. So He can't be everywhere at the same time because that's not what human natures do. So Calvin isn't going with what's revealed. He, and some Calvinists today, are going with some type of logic or of some definition that says humanity cannot do this.

Well, when it's the God-man, and there's this communication of attributes, then we take all those limitations off because now we're just receiving what God says. So, yeah, they have this idea that Jesus can't be bodily present in the bread and the wine; and we say, "Nah, that's not what the Bible says. I mean, clearly Jesus said it, and He's

68 See Calvin, *Institutes*, Book 4, chapter 17.

communicating these attributes. So that's the truth. So that's that."

Lastly, Calvin said that in some type of way at the Supper, through the Spirit, we ascend to heaven by the power of the Holy Spirit. It's interesting that he has a category for us as limited creatures ascending in some type of way to heaven, but then Jesus can't do what He says? Just seems to be some other type of motivation there to preserve or protect something else as opposed to going with what is revealed. But that's what we should do as Christians: put ourselves to the side and go with what Jesus says, what the Bible says, because the Bible is the ultimate authority, and that's what we submit to.

So, man, this was a weighty topic, but shout-out to Dr. David Maxwell again for that article, which I used heavily as an outline for my arguments above. I think this is very helpful. So check it out; walk through it slowly. I tried to go through it at a decent pace, but I know it's a lot. It could be kind of overwhelming.

So anyway, that's that. Jesus Christ is distributed and received in the Sacrament. Through bread and wine, He literally enters the bodies and lives of those who commune. This is wonderful news for those who believe in Him. Almighty God dwells with us. He comes in a tangible, concrete form. We know that He has come to us when we commune because He promises to do this. The bodily presence of Christ is a powerful comfort and assurance in times of trial. It is a source of strength in adversity. Whatever our situation, we know that Christ comes to us.

And I love this because of the practicality of it. I mean, when you talk about living in a fallen world, being a broken and sinful person, Jesus says, "I want to give you a sure way of knowing that I'm with you. I want to give you a sure, concrete, tangible way so that you can see with your eyes, hold with your hands, taste with your taste buds My forgiveness." And He does that, and the church has drawn on these teachings in the darkest times.

Think about the Christians in the Colosseum. We all have heard about those moments when our brothers and sisters were being tortured by animals and ripped apart. Those Christians were holding on to these realities. They could say, "I know for sure that based on Jesus' Word and regularly communing with Him that He is with me. He's literally with me. I have received His body and blood."

And today, we can do the same thing. Whether you're going through a struggle, a loss, or a low point in life, you can know every time you receive the bread and wine that Jesus is present bodily, that He's with you. You can have that comfort. That's the point. And ultimately, we receive the forgiveness of sin. We can know that our sins are forgiven.

So we're not walking around nervous, thinking, *Man, maybe God doesn't forgive me, maybe He's mad at me.* When we receive His body and blood, we receive that comfort as we move out into the world. And that's part of the sweet reality that gets lost on us when we dismiss this as just a symbolic meal.

So I pray that the Holy Spirit will lead His church back to the essence of His words that comfort us in the Lord's Supper. Beautiful.

> **What's more, he comes to us with his promised forgiveness. The same body, once crucified for us and now risen and glorified, is our food. In his institution of the Lord's Supper, Jesus said that the blood that we drink was poured out for the forgiveness of sins (Matthew 26:28). Our Savior promises his grace**

> whenever we receive this sacrament in faith.
>
> In addition to this vertical relationship with God, the Lord's Supper also has a horizontal aspect. While Jesus Christ personally comes to each person who communes, this is not a private dinner for two; it is a banquet shared with others.[69]

Beautiful. I love that.

69 Steven P. Mueller, ed., *Called to Believe, Teach, and Confess: An Introduction to Doctrinal Theology* (Wipf and Stock Publishers, 2005), 355.

CHAPTER 7
RESPONDING THROUGH THE ARTS

To share what I've learned, I thought it only right to do so using the arts and music. In my project titled *Neo Ethos*, I sought to provide somewhat of a timeline to track the events of early Christianity on American soil. Prior to creating the album, I asked myself how we got here. How did we get the version of Christianity that we have now? One that has dismissed the Sacraments as mere symbols, which has led to a more me-centered expression of Christianity. The album is an effort to answer those questions.

My premise is that the overthrowing of the Sacraments left a void in the church. The natural space in our hearts or in our Christian experience to connect with God through His ordained means and to unite with something bigger than ourselves was left empty. Nevertheless, we continued to have unfed appetites for a supernatural encounter with our Creator. Since the Sacraments were stripped of their relevance in our everyday understanding of the faith, in our joys and sufferings, we then sought to have that void filled by other things like high church attendance and church growth programs, misuses of the gifts of the Holy Spirit, down to borrowing from Eastern religions. All in an effort to experience something transcendent. I've heard more Christians talk about burning sage, manifestations, affirmations, and curiosity concerning ancestral encounters lately than I ever have before.

It appears to me that we desire to belong to something that's greater than a mere social community. We want to think about those who have died in Christ (ancestors) as still being relevant somehow. With us, even. We don't know that the Lord's Supper unites us with those who are present with the Lord but no longer with us. We have been tricked out of our ancient Christian heritage and sold the lies of Gnosticism, which teaches material is evil and beneath God's station to use in His plan of salvation. Therefore, many reject Jesus' bodily presence in the bread and the wine for the forgiveness of sins. Many have allowed themselves permission to align with the enlightenment and to be skeptical about truth claims that we cannot test in a laboratory, such as the real presence of Christ in the Meal.

Therefore, I composed an album to walk my audience through the chain of events that led up to contemporary Christianity. Let's consider my song "1525," which recounts the first "rebaptism." Of which there is no such thing. Paul is clear in Ephesians 4:5: "One Lord, one faith, one baptism."

"1525" (featuring Dr. Cameron MacKenzie)

Verse 1

Something is missing / Feel like the village went vacant / Like it's been pillaged in a revolt from all the peasants / Even the Scriptures were cut and pasted / Missing pages / Something is different left all the laws and regulations / We call them radicals / Some of them revolutionaries / Let's call them Anabaptist / "Rebaptizers" / Man that's scary / January1525 / Felix Manz / Had a visit /

In his kitchen where it all began / George Blaurock, Conrad Grebel they all connected / Rejected biblical Baptism's message / And started spreading it / Now here we are / At further distance from our ancient faith / A metaphor / Is how we speak of His amazing grace / Help us, Lord.

Hook

Something's really missing, oh my God! / Oh my God! (repeat 3 times)

Feel like I'm back from 1525!

Something's really missing, oh my God! (repeat 2 times)

This is trippy trippy odd / This is wild / Oh my God!

Verse 2

Some Protestants have now added burdens with blurred lines / Sweet Sacraments / Overthrown or undermined / Excessive fruit checking like Adam in the Garden of Eden / Ignore God / Heed the serpent / Then we start eatin' / A lot of sermons in pulpits [sound] like a Gnostic wrote them /

A lot of Scripture quoted / But symbolism gets emoted / This dude assumed that I went to visit the Vatican / Came back with vestments / Stressing the Sacraments / But that's not the case just being accurate / Preserving our faith protected by Africans / Eastern fathers / Europeans / We've got a whole heritage / Evangelicals disparage / And label you a heretic / Help us, God.

Hook

This next song calls to the forefront the reality that decisions were made for us concerning the old way, the way of ancient Christianity that the church fathers presented. It invites us to be made aware and then to participate in the recovery of the sacramental life for the sake of better serving our generation's needs from a place of unity as a church, solidarity in doctrine, and energy in meeting needs.

"We Ain't Even Know"

Verse 1

Everything you think Roman Catholic you're trained to reject / It's a shame 'cause your timeline's backwards / And your interpretation came afterwards / Raised in the West / In America / Influenced by the Baptists / It's a reason we don't wear crucifixes / With Jesus on the cross bleeding / Or even baptize infants / They say public professions conversions and such / Before you're accepted in the church is a must / It's a reason we don't value tradition that much / Decisions that shifted like stick in the clutch / Traditions that came in particular Baptists / With their interpretation of particular chapters.

Hook

Decisions got made for us bro / We ain't even know / We ain't even know about it sis / Matter of fact / We didn't exist / But now you know / Please can you be a part of the convo / Say you got no type of affiliation / Say you a part nondenomination / Say you only focus on salvation / You 'bout debate on separation / I get / Trust me / You're Baptist / Let me cook though.

Verse 2

What's the point / Why I'm so lit / Why I ain't rapping 'bout the things I was saying back in '06 / 'Cause I learned there was a lot missed / Not everything /

But important things that the church flipped / For example certain verses / That communicate gift / That we turned into work it's / Tied to the Arbella ship / That carried over Christians that switched up the Eucharist / That ferried over to this land for emancipation / And religious freedom don't need toleration / Scared by the papacy and Charles the Second / The one who had John Bunyan thrown into prison / Vestments / Candles / Anglican culture / The Christian calendar / The liturgy / They over it / That whole ethos / Many tossing it over / Now here we are / Repeating back / Only what they told us.

Hook

Hear ye! Hear ye! The secret is out! This song is a public cry. A public service announcement, if you will. As I stand on my soapbox yelling to the masses that those who influenced early American religious life, those who threw out the baby with the bathwater, brought with them a vendetta. A vendetta that had lingering consequences on the church. Now we are reaping from what they sowed: a somewhat hollow expression of Christianity. Yes, God is still building His church, which says more about His faithfulness than ours.

"Secret Is Out"

Hook

The secret is out the people have heard / Preacher been tweaking the Word / From Puritan Separatist / Down to the Methodist / Yes I can back it with Word / The message been meddled with / Colonial settlement / But He still building the church / What Jesus established they think is absurd / Dismissing the visible Word.

Verse 1

I took you Marburg remember the colloquy / Zwingli and Luther did not agree / Not on the meaning of is / Now how it impacted the thirteen colonies / Anabaptist then to John Calvin / Reformation making waves / Made its way over to England to Anglicans are made by Henry the Eighth / Out of that your Puritans / Eventually some of them separated / Then they travel to the "New World" / Eventually even the Quakers made it / Then to Baptist / To Wesley / To Whitfield / Edwards and the Great Awakenings / Then the Restoration

Movements happened / Pentecostals then the Black Baptist / Civil Rights it went to A.M.E. African Methodist Episcopal / Like Zwingli reducing the visible Word / Americas made them a symbol too / Pitiful.

Hook

Verse 2

Now lest you think because souls were saved / And the church expanded / That's evidence / It's never meant what set precedence / Because of its prevalence / Means it's heaven sent / God can take our five loaves and our two fish and feed five thousand / God can even make a donkey speak / Or the rocks cry out if we gon' doubt Him / God is faithful when we ain't faithful / How we made a metaphor of the Lord's Table / Plus we on this side of history / So we disagree with the interpretation / Of the saints in majority / On American soil / And every other nation / The consequence is / We're constantly fruit checking / People living under condemnation / They say / You believe in consubstantiation / I say nah / That is not a combination / That Jesus explained in the Bible pages / Therefore it's not a part of our conversation.

Hook

"My Side" is a heartfelt song meant to encourage all who mourn the loss of what the church lost. What she suffers as a result of being damaged by those who struck off the sacramental limbs of the body for the sake of convenience and ridding themselves of papal and Anglican rule. This tune touches the soul and reminds us that we have God's Word on our side, and history vouches for God's Word. It encourages us to stand firm and to not get weary in doing good.

"My Side" (featuring V. Rose)

Hook

History on my side / Bible on my side / Scripture on my side / Bible on my side / History on my side / History on my side / Scripture on my side / Bible on my side / Scripture on my side / Scripture on my side / Scripture on my side / Scripture on my side / Bible on my side / Bible on my side / Bible on my side / Bible on my side

Verse 1

He said, Flame, these seem like nonessentials / Not even honorable mention if I'm honest with you /

And issue of the conscience that's not consequential / At best they feel divisive from the fundamentals / Baggage from Roman Catholics that Luther never severed / Devil use you to take us backwards / Woo / Took him back to Bible pages / Greek and Hebrew / Aramaic / Took him straight to Jesus' statements / Before the denomination Roman Catholic had existed / Polycarp / Even Clement / Then extended through Patristics / Body parts have been missing / Zwingli swinging the pendulum / Calvin carried his sentiments / Sacraments salvific instruments / Got witness.

Hook

Verse 2

Whether Irenaeus Against Heresies / All the way to Hermann Sasse / We gon' plenty heed / The Eucharistic promise that when we receive / Consecrated bread and wine / the body / Blood received / And we gon' baptize our babies / 'Cause it's God who does the saving / Water / Word / That's how we say it / See it's God who does the verbs / Does the drowning when submerged / Does the rising like the third to us / The Bible never says it's just an outward sign / Of an inward change / You ain't gonna find it / Went to check / It ain't nowhere in the text / That bread and wine / They just simply represent / What I got?

Hook

"This Is Christianity" is an anthem for all those who have preserved the ancient creeds, even where it's not popular. It's a reminder to the church of who we are. It's a call for us to lean in and not to be afraid to be the baptized of the Lord. To resist the pressure from contemporary renditions of the faith that have obscured or outright denied the heritage that carried us here and that will stand the test of time.

"This Is Christianity" (featuring Dr. Gerhard Bode)

Verse 1

It's not by my moral conduct when my life runs out of time / Was I standing on my business by His righteousness or mine / Was I trying to justify myself all by myself or nah / Did I believe in Him by Baptism Ephesians 4 and 5? / Oh my God / I know / Apart from / Christ I'm / Slime / You say / You no sin / Then you just / Lying / Even Nicene

Creed said it / Water and Word is how we get it / Many martyrs got beheaded / Believe the Lord you won't regret it.

Hook

What is this what is this / One Lord / What is this what is this / One faith / What is this what is this / One Baptism / What is this what is this / No chaser. (repeat 2 times)

This is this is Christianity / Father / Son / The Spirit Trinity / God-bearer through virginity / Bore the Son in His divinity / Bore the Son in His humanity / Sent to save us from our vanity / Baptism for remission of / Sin / This is Christianity.

Verse 2

See "we hold that one is justified by faith apart from all the works of the Law" / This the essence and our Christian message we made a mess they sent Christ to the cross / The carnal mind says to walk in the flesh / That we can please God by our good deeds / We're sin-sick please send us a Savior / To save us from trying to save ourselves please /

That's the disease / That's the disease / Original sin / Yes that's the disease / And our actual sin where we actively sin is a manifestation of the way we're conceived / Sweet the taste is the grace of our God / God the Father who sent us His Son / To reconcile the world unto Himself / Through Word and Sacraments / That's how it's done.

Hook

"Another Man's Shoes" is a song rooted in the harsh reality that though we may mean well and innocently want people to experience the joy and freedom of the Gospel, some will only hear what they want to hear. In this song, I liken myself to Dr. Martin Luther, who thought the masses would celebrate his discoveries but found much resistance, to his surprise. It's a relatable song that reminds the church that though we may come under attack by the devil, to remember 1 John 4:4:

> **Little children, you are from God and have overcome them, for He who is in you is greater than he who is in the world.**

"Another Man's Shoes" (featuring Deezle, Vadé, J Hott)

Hook

Sometimes we win sometimes we lose / With the choices we all choose / But you'll know until you / Walk in another man's shoes / You may think it's what you know / What you thought you thought fasho / Until you walk in / Another man's shoes.

Verse 1

So you wanna walk in these based on what you see / Huh / Measuring yourself up against me / They ain't gon' fit your feet / Nah / It's scary how very often / Can barely carry my crosses / I've buried so many coffins / I'm weak / But all you see / Are the brightest moments / Viral moments / Make you wanna live just like it, don't it / But let me invite you inside this moment / It's like all the lights were off and the whole system switched up charging cost / It's like doing our penance and paying for indulgences that our Christ got lost / So I put my neck on the line / They put a price on my head / They sent their hitters to slide / I hit the tower and hid / Salute to Frederick the Wise / But I'm trusting the Spirit of God / I'm preaching the Gospel then closing my eyes / I opened them up and then both of my daughters had died / GOD!

Hook

Verse 2

I could've stayed silent / I ain't have to make a real big deal about it / But I couldn't stay silent / While faith is attacked by Satan the tyrant / Guess that makes me a marked man / Marcus Gray see a warrior walked in / Through my momma named Carolyn Gray and my daddy named Sam and they're both in the Lord's hands / While I'm still on this earth / Dealing with hurt in my feelings at first / Why would You take them from me back-to-back / How does an only child handle that / Knowing there chapters that we hadn't closed / How could You end the story on the lows / End it on the highs / When a Christian dies / We're incentivized / Heaven gives us hope / But they see the Grammy nomination and the compensation hitting stages with the gang /

But when you push ancient Christianity through Word and Sacrament then you see people change / DANG! / I really thought they would hallelujah / The closest to ya will cock-and-shoot ya / Standing too close to Dr. Luther.

Hook

As Christians who are united with our brothers and sisters from the generations before us, we must be bold in holding to what the Bible teaches and follow in the line of those who faithfully confessed it.

CHAPTER 8

LIVING LIKE THE EARLY CHURCH

The true nature of the Eucharist is a hill worth dying on. It is the peak of the spirituality we seek. It is the height of the nearness to God that we desire. It provides the full panorama of hope that we long for. In it, God has addressed our past problem with original sin, inherited from our first parents, Adam and Eve. He addresses our present problem with indwelling sin, our future fears and anxiety tied to our inability to control the future, and the reality that death awaits us all.

The early church was so overwhelmingly aware of these realities that they did not think of the gathering of the church as simply a time to hear a relevant sermon or to get inspired to be a better person. They rightly understood that when Christians gathered, they came together to commune with Jesus Himself. Heaven and earth joined during the gathering. Not only did they believe that the church gathered but also that the angels were there as well as those who had fallen asleep in Christ Jesus. All those who belonged to Jesus' Body, the church, are present at the Sacrament of the Altar.

This is an entirely different motivation to gather with the family of God if you are anticipating fellowship with the entire host of heaven alongside sisters and brothers in the faith. One would not assume they can regularly skip out on meeting together with the saints if they knew exactly what was taking place week after week. This should make the gathering a joyfully anticipated time.

A person once told me that she was no longer growing at her church. In fact, she believed that she had outgrown her church because she was learning more away from church than on Sunday mornings. With the help of podcasts, sermon series, and Bible study material, she concluded that she had little to no need to meet on Sundays. This person said she got regular fellowship with a few good Christians who all linked up at their houses and talked about theology and Scripture. She went on to share how meaningful it was because they could go deeper into theology with one another than the pastor was willing to go on Sunday mornings. Therefore, sleeping in on most Sundays was permissible and understandable. Or waking up on Sundays to do such things in bed was sufficient too.

When gathering together gets reduced down to simply singing and hearing from a man who has less Bible knowledge than you might have, I can understand why you would be tempted to skip out on it altogether. If Sunday morning no longer "challenges" you, I can see why you would conclude that you can just wake up on Sunday morning, pop on a podcast from a scholar, and "have church" by yourself or with your family alone. If the Lord's Supper is merely a symbolic meal, then why celebrate it regularly? It doesn't do anything but provide another way of using your mind to think deeply about what Jesus did for you on the cross. You can do that at home or anywhere. According to that person, he does that all day anyway. He lives in a perpetual state of communion and therefore gets that itch scratched elsewhere.

John Chrysostom talked about the Eucharist in the most relevant of ways:

> **Nor do we in vain make mention of the departed in the course of the divine mysteries, and approach God in their behalf, beseeching the Lamb Who is before**

us, Who taketh away the sins of the world . . . that some refreshment may thereby ensue to them.[70]

Gathered around the body and bread on Sundays or whenever the church communes together was rightly understood as a meeting of not only the living but also those who had departed. What a beautiful comfort this is for anyone whose loved ones are now gathered with the Lord. Think of people who have lost spouses, parents, children, siblings, and the like. They all meet together when heaven and earth meet at the Lord's Table. Chrysostom gave to God's church such wonderful truths. These are the teachings that sustained us as the Body of believers since the beginning.

Ignatius longs for the Meal because in it he knows we receive our dear Lord and Savior. It is not an afterthought to him. Not a thing he can do without. The Meal is "incorruptible love."[71] No mere meal can be described as such. It is clearly a mystery being acknowledged here, a reality that stirs Ignatius up toward longing. This is the way God's Spirit instructed him to teach the church because Jesus taught it in His Word.

There is such a sacred nature to the rite that it was guarded by the church and not haphazardly distributed. Justin Martyr warns that no one should be "allowed to partake"[72] in the Lord's Supper without believing the teachings about it.

The church rightly understood that the Eucharist was central to the Christian's life. In fact, it was the core and the heart of it, along with Baptism. This was the case because Jesus established the

70 Chrysostom, *Homilies on First Corinthians*, Homily 41, paragraph 8 (*NPNF1* 12:253).

71 Ignatius, *Epistle to the Romans*, chapter 7 (*ANF* 1:77).

72 *The First Apology of Justin*, chapter 66 (*ANF* 1:185).

Supper. He is the one who told the church to partake repeatedly. He is the one who attached a mystery and a promise to the partaking of bread and wine. He in fact is the one who made it a Sacrament, which is an earthly element joined to God's Word to deliver what it points to. That is in fact what the mystery entails. How can these earthly elements remind us of Jesus' body and blood and at the same time be the body and blood? Because that's what Jesus gave us. He fashioned it and charged us to happily enjoy it. To participate in it and be blessed.

It should not be understood as magic. No. Yes, there is a mystical union taking place at the communion rail, but the benefits are received by faith. As one lays hold of the truths Jesus reveals during the gathering, one then is blessed with these gifts. There is no replacement for this. It cannot be forgone for a private devotional on Sunday morning on an app on your phone. Are there occasions when persons cannot gather? Sure. Are there emergency situations that prevent people from participating with the community of saints? Absolutely. And a good shepherd will make sure to bring those delightful gifts to accommodate such circumstances. Yet on typical occasions, affairs should be conducted in the manner in which Jesus lays out—as often as the Body gathers.

The early church saw the Eucharist as their identity. It united them together across the spectrum. Whether you were wealthy or impoverished. A bondservant or freed. Well educated or unlearned. As one who receives Jesus into your body, you are made one, equal, and personally loved by the Savior who joins you together regularly with fellow family members and the host of heaven. This becomes the driving force for reconciliation among bickering sects. If you have a falling out with someone, you are reminded at the rail that

Christ has reconciled you in Himself, and if you are in Him, then you are conjoined with the one with whom you are at odds. The Meal strengthens your faith to end your grudge, to shed your drive for revenge. God's Spirit gives you a holy push to embrace your loved one, who is united with you in Christ at the Lord's Table.

I oftentimes make this statement: I hold to "ancient Christianity as preserved through confessional Lutheran thought." I hope it's becoming abundantly clear why I use it so much. It is not meant to communicate that contemporary Christianity has nothing good to offer the church. Not at all. It is clear to me that contemporary expressions of Christianity have contributed much good. Many of us are a by-product of it. I love how seriously the modern church takes reaching the lost, meeting them where they are, as we say. Another skill is taking seemingly lofty concepts and making them digestible to a social media–driven culture. Even in scholarship, there are helpful thoughts being written and discussed that benefit today's concerns, tailoring ancient truths for present-day issues and hang-ups. For that I am grateful.

Nevertheless, I use the phrase because on matters of maintaining and preserving the essence of the faith once and for all delivered to the saints, contemporary expressions are at risk of straying further. Some even question the Nicene Creed because it contains the phrase "I acknowledge one Baptism for the remission of sins." What a scary thing to gamble with. While I was studying in seminary, learning more about the church fathers, I simultaneously was being called to notice what confessional Lutherans believe about it all. I was happy to notice that the rhetoric from Luther and his cohorts reverberated the words and writings of the earliest texts and treatises on matters of church life, church teaching, and the priorities and emphases of the church. I came across Dr. Luther's own works, where he illustrated his earnest desire to hold fast to the apostles' teachings and be a successor of the doctrines they espoused, putting forth nothing new that would change the fabric of the faith. Only clarifying what was there, hidden, or buried. He says this of the Holy Meal:

> *How can bodily eating and drinking do such great things?* Certainly not just eating and drinking do these things, but the words written here: "Given and shed for you for the forgiveness of sins." These words, along with the bodily eating and drinking, are the main thing in the Sacrament. Whoever believes these words has exactly what they say: "forgiveness of sins."[73]

> The heart cannot eat it physically nor can the mouth eat it spiritually.[74]

> I believe and do not doubt, and shall also with the help and grace of my dear Lord Jesus Christ adhere to this confession until the last day, that where mass is celebrated according to Christ's ordinance, be it among us Lutherans or under the papacy or in Greece or in India . . . nevertheless, under the form of bread, the true body of Christ, given for us on the cross, under the form of wine, the true blood of Christ, shed for us, are present; furthermore, it

73 Small Catechism, Sacrament of the Altar. Emphasis in original.

74 *That These Words of Christ* (AE 37:93).

> is not a spiritual or imagined body and blood but the genuine natural body and blood derived from the holy, virginal, true, human body of Mary, conceived without a human body by the Holy Spirit alone. This body and blood of Christ are even now sitting at the right hand of God in majesty, in the divine person called Jesus Christ, who is a genuine, true, eternal God with the Father of whom he was born from eternity, etc. This body and this blood of the Son of God, Jesus Christ, not only the holy and worthy but also sinners and the unworthy truly administer and receive bodily, although invisibly, with their hands, their mouths, the chalice, paten, corporal, and whatever they use for this purpose when it is administered and received in the mass.
>
> This is my faith; this I know, and no one shall wrest it from me.[75]

Hear the words of Philip Melanchthon, who contributed greatly to the Lutheran Confessions:

> Article X has been approved, in which we confess the following: We believe that in the Lord's Supper Christ's body and blood are truly and substantially present and are truly administered with those things that are seen (bread and wine) to those who

75 A Letter of Dr. Martin Luther Concerning His Book on the Private Mass (AE 38:224).

> **receive the Sacrament. We constantly defend this belief, as the subject has been carefully examined and considered. Since Paul says, "The bread that we break, is it not a participation in the body of Christ?" (1 Corinthians 10:16), it would follow that if the Lord's body were not truly present, the bread is not a communion of the body, but only of the Christ's spirit. We have determined that not only the Roman Church affirms Christ's bodily presence. The Greek Church also now believes, and formerly believed, the same.[76]**

I was trained under such a narrow and tight understanding of who was really saved, to only consider "professors of faith," which is a term meant to shade a person's claim to faith. It heaps skepticism and doubt on a person until they can earn approval by appearing righteous consistently. Granted, a Christian should be marked by a new ethic that reflects their Baptism and their identity in Christ. Amen.

The problem was utilizing arbitrary measures to determine where a person stood with Christ. The answer was almost always a no if these questions were asked: "Are Roman Catholics saved?" "Are the Orthodox churches Christian?" Working through church history softened my heart. I realized that though there are blaring disagreements between confessional Lutherans, the Orthodox churches, and Roman Catholicism, we nonetheless agree on the Gospel of Jesus' bodily presence at the Eucharist, rooted in Jesus' earthly ministry and delivering that same flesh and blood for the forgiveness of sins.

76 Apology of the Augsburg Confession, Article 10, paragraphs 54–55.

I rejoiced greatly after learning of the commonalities we shared with other older traditions of the church.

May God continue to unite His church using the commonality of what we do agree on concerning the mystical union of the Sacraments. May He foster healthy dialogue among the universal church, resulting in a strong body. Indeed, Jesus' own Body functioning in the world, doing much good without restraint. As Paul declares in Galatians 5:22–23:

> **But the fruit of the Spirit is love, joy, peace, patience, kindness, goodness, faithfulness, gentleness, self-control; against such things there is no law.**

For this reason, I plead with "my kinsmen according to the flesh" (Romans 9:3) who are researching the origins of Christianity and discovering Africa's major role in the Holy Spirit's story. Please resist the magnetic temptation to reference older African traditions simply to dignify Blackness. For God has already given dignity to you and in Christ Jesus, our Lord, who died for a multiethnic Bride. May we not use Christianity's African heritage without careful consideration of the theology of ancient African Christians, particularly concerning Baptism and the Lord's Supper. If we are going to "deconstruct" and then "reconstruct," may we do so with honesty and integrity. May we visit the writings of the early church and the early creeds to better understand our ancient faith and the sacramental life of our African ancestors. May we honor them in the way I'm sure they would be most honored: by holding the Gospel of Christ, our Lord, together with His instituted means, Baptism and the Lord's Supper.

For this reason I am beyond moved and elated to confess the same sweet baptismal realities that comforted our dear African sisters in the faith, Perpetua and Felicitas. They were martyrs who in AD 203 were mangled and mutilated, first by gladiators and then by savage beasts. These two brave mothers gave each other a holy Christian kiss of peace before being executed by the sword. They were certain that in Baptism, God, in Christ Jesus, washes away sins (Acts 22:16), grants His Holy Spirit, and marks us as His daughters and sons.

CHAPTER 9

A PRAYER

I declare and pray:

- That this generation will learn about ancient Christianity and the history of Jesus' Bride.
- That this generation will learn to rightly understand the word of truth (2 Timothy 2:15), correctly dividing between Law and Gospel.
- That this generation will recover the reality of God's delivery system through Word and Sacrament, a thing Satan stole from us through zealous men lacking knowledge.
- That this generation will proclaim the universal nature of Jesus' atonement. That He indeed died for all without exception. That by faith, one apprehends Christ and all that He won for us in His earthly ministry.
- That this generation will thrive in the joy and task of vocation. That as we function as God's hands and feet, the Lord hides Himself in us and cares for the world. That He uses us to answer prayers through diverse acts of service, sacrifice, and wholesome living.

- That this generation will contend for the faith once and for all delivered to the saints—both against those outside and inside our beloved faith—and that this be done with love, respect, and kindness, but nonetheless with boldness.
- That this generation will enjoy the arts and create beautiful things so as to adorn the world and the work God has entrusted to us—to indeed relieve burdens and enhance the happiness of others.
- That this generation will ever so gently pursue those who have left the faith and are crushed in spirit, to pray for them earnestly and continuously, and to repaint the picture of God according to Scripture rightly understood, that they may reimagine their loving Father and grasp for Him. He is near with outstretched arms of reconciliation.

Amen.

ACKNOWLEDGMENTS

Thank you to Rev. Dr. Joel C. Elowsky, Rev. Dr. David R. Maxwell, Rev. Dr. Charles P. Arand, Dr. Erik Herrmann, and Rev. Dr. Paul W. Robinson for exposing me to the church fathers and for opening up a beautiful world of church history that would have remained closed to me otherwise. My gratitude cannot be measured.

APPENDIX: CREEDS

The Nicene Creed (written in AD 325)

I believe in one God, the Father Almighty, maker of heaven and earth and of all things visible and invisible.

And in one Lord Jesus Christ, the only-begotten Son of God, begotten of His Father before all worlds, God of God, Light of Light, very God of very God, begotten, not made, being of one substance with the Father, by whom all things were made; who for us men and for our salvation came down from heaven and was incarnate by the Holy Spirit of the virgin Mary and was made man; and was crucified also for us under Pontius Pilate. He suffered and was buried. And the third day He rose again according to the Scriptures and ascended into heaven and sits at the right hand of the Father. And He will come again with glory to judge the living and the dead, whose kingdom shall have no end.

And I believe in the Holy Spirit, the Lord and Giver of Life, who proceeds from the Father and the Son, who with the Father and the Son together is worshiped and glorified, who spoke by the prophets. And I believe in one holy Christian and apostolic

Church, I acknowledge one Baptism for the remission of sins, and I look for the resurrection of the dead and the life of the world to come. Amen.

The Athanasian Creed (written in the fifth or sixth century)

Written against the Arians.

Whosoever desires to be saved must, above all, hold the catholic faith.

Whoever does not keep it whole and undefiled will without doubt perish eternally.

And the catholic faith is this,

that we worship one God in Trinity and Trinity in unity, neither confusing the persons nor dividing the substance.

For the Father is one person, the Son is another, and the Holy Spirit is another.

But the Godhead of the Father and of the Son and of the Holy Spirit is one: the glory equal, the majesty coeternal.

Such as the Father is, such is the Son, and such is the Holy Spirit:

the Father uncreated, the Son uncreated, the Holy Spirit uncreated;

the Father infinite, the Son infinite, the Holy Spirit infinite;

the Father eternal, the Son eternal, the Holy Spirit eternal.

And yet there are not three Eternals, but one Eternal,

just as there are not three Uncreated or three Infinites, but one Uncreated and one Infinite.

In the same way, the Father is almighty, the Son almighty, the Holy Spirit almighty;

and yet there are not three Almighties but one Almighty.

So the Father is God, the Son is God, the Holy Spirit is God;

and yet there are not three Gods, but one God.

So the Father is Lord, the Son is Lord, the Holy Spirit is Lord;

and yet there are not three Lords, but one Lord.

Just as we are compelled by the Christian truth to acknowledge each distinct person as God and Lord,

so also are we prohibited by the catholic religion to say that there are three Gods or Lords.

The Father is not made nor created nor begotten by anyone. The Son is neither made nor created, but begotten of the Father alone.

The Holy Spirit is of the Father and of the Son, neither made nor created nor begotten but proceeding.

Thus, there is one Father, not three Fathers; one Son, not three Sons; one Holy Spirit, not three Holy Spirits.

And in this Trinity none is before or after another; none is greater or less than another;

but the whole three persons are coeternal with each other and coequal so that in all things, as has been stated above, the Trinity in Unity and Unity in Trinity is to be worshiped.

Therefore, whoever desires to be saved must think thus of the Trinity.

But it is also necessary for everlasting salvation that one faithfully believe the incarnation of our Lord Jesus Christ.

Therefore, it is the right faith that we believe and confess that our Lord Jesus Christ, the Son of God, is at the same time both God and man.

He is God, begotten from the substance of the Father before all ages; and He is man, born from the substance of His mother in this age:

perfect God and perfect man, composed of a rational soul and human flesh;

equal to the Father with respect to His divinity, less

than the Father with respect to His humanity.

Although He is God and man, He is not two, but one Christ:

one, however, not by the conversion of the divinity into flesh but by assumption of the humanity into God;

one altogether, not by confusion of substance, but by unity of person.

For as the rational soul and flesh is one man, so God and man is one Christ,

who suffered for our salvation, descended into hell, rose again on the third day from the dead,

ascended into heaven, and is seated at the right hand of the Father, from whence He will come to judge the living and the dead.

At His coming all people will rise again with their bodies and give an account concerning their own deeds.

And those who have done good will enter into eternal life, and those who have done evil into eternal fire.

This is the catholic faith; whoever does not believe it faithfully and firmly cannot be saved.